Making **WREATHS**
FOR ALL SEASONS

Making WREATHS
for All Seasons

Pamela Westland

CREATIVE HOMEOWNER PRESS®

A QUINTET BOOK

Creative Homeowner Press
24 Park Way
Upper Saddle River, New Jersey 07458

CREATIVE HOMEOWNER PRESS and
colophons are registered trademarks of
Federal Marketing Corporation.

Printed in Singapore

LC: 93-71772
ISBN: 1-880029-25-1

CONTENTS

INTRODUCTION

Making wreaths and garlands to decorate our homes and places of worship has its origins in ancient cultures all around the world. Long before people "arranged" flowers in the way we now understand the term, they composed garlands of flowers and leaves and festooned their holy places in an act of worship, and their homes as a symbol of good luck. It is clear from early wall paintings and sculptures that wreaths, especially those composed of roses and other aromatic plants, were used as door and wall decorations, and in Greek and Roman times, laurel wreaths were presented as a symbol of victory and honor.

The practice of creating these decorations has survived the ages, although the symbolism has gradually changed. Wreaths, which may be hung on the front door, or on an interior door or wall are considered a sign of friendship and welcome; indeed, the evergreen wreath that is traditionally hung on the door at Christmastime is known as a welcome wreath.

Garlands, festoons, swags, floral ribbons, call them what you will, are appreciated for their purely decorative qualities, and set the scene for religious festivals and family celebrations alike. A garland of glossy evergreens outlining the fireplace at Christmas, a swag of pale-colored summery flowers draped across the bridal table at a wedding reception, and a floral ribbon encircling a church pillar or spanning a window have close links with those early floral garlands.

The range of decorative materials you can use in such designs is as varied as your imagination will allow: the luxury of fresh flowers that gladden each successive season; the long-lasting beauty of dried and preserved flowers, foliage and seed heads; the vibrant colors and complementary shapes of fruit and vegetables; the wayward outlines of dried twigs and branches; the shiny roundness of nuts and the heady aroma of herbs and spices all have a decorative part to play. The structures on which wreaths and garlands may be composed are many and varied, too, with grasses, supple stems and twigs, wire, cord, rope, string, moss, sweet-smelling hay and preshaped plastic foam among them.

If you want to create wreaths and garlands as part of a decorative setting for a special occasion, to compose a design in romantic mood, or you simply want to express joy in the season, be it the onset of

spring or the height of summer, you will find ideas throughout this book to delight and inspire you. Together with each series of step-by-step photographs you will find a list of the plant materials, tools and holding materials used in the creation of that design. But you should not feel constrained by the suggestions we make and the flowers and leaves we have used. You will soon see how easy it is to adapt each design to your own requirements, preferences and color

LEFT *These are some of the materials used in the composition of the wreaths and garlands featured in the book.*

1 *nasturtiums*
2 *thick cord*
3 *string*
4 *twine*
5 *clear all-purpose glue*
6 *microwave-dried cornflowers*
7 *heavy gauge wire*
8 *roll of fine silver wire*
9 *medium-gauge stub wires*
10 *fine silver wires*
11 *flower scissors*
12 *wire cutters*

schemes, using our suggestions as a springboard for your own creative ability.

To help you make the very best of your creations, and to derive the maximum pleasure from each one, there is a section on harvesting, selecting, and treating flowers and foliage of all kinds, and on drying and preserving techniques, including the use of a microwave. A further section assesses the color and textural values of a range of plant materials and explains how you can combine them to advantage in your designs: and another section is devoted entirely to the practicalities. Here you will find a detailed explanation of the materials needed, and the methods you can use to create the wreaths and garlands of your choice.

These decorative styles, which have delighted our ancestors for centuries, are as relevant now as they have ever been. And, as we hope our ideas will indicate, their design potential knows no bounds.

Getting Started

CHAPTER 1

NATURAL PLANT MATERIALS

A colorful table-center ring arranged with fresh-as-a-bright-spring-morning flowers in celebration of the Easter festival; a sweetly scented wreath of herbs and other aromatic plants gathered at the height of summer; a heart-shaped twig ring decorated with dried roses, a romantic gift for someone you love; a swag of sun-bleached cereals and grasses, highlighted with vibrant dried flowers; or a glossy evergreen garland for Christmas, enriched and embellished with seasonal fruits, berries, and woody cones – whatever your choice of decoration, they all have one requirement in common: the materials you use, whether they are fresh or dried, must be in perfect condition, so that they will be worthy of the care and attention to be lavished on them. Every flower and leaf, seed head and cone will have its part to play in the finished design, and must be able to withstand the appraisal and admiring glances that are due to it.

Making wreaths and rings, garlands and swags of natural plant materials imposes no restrictions at all on the materials you can use. The limitations are only in the form and shape the designs may take. But even then, as we hope the projects in this book will show, there is plenty of scope for lively imagination and lateral thinking.

Fresh flowers of all kinds have a long tradition of use in such designs, and bring a joyful, spur-of-the-moment feeling that is hard to achieve with preserved materials. From the slenderest of wayside flowers –

ABOVE *Dried flowers in waiting – even before they are arranged, dried flowers make a delightful composition with their clear, bright colors and variety of textures. Those in the basket include peonies, sea lavender, quaking grass, love-in-a-mist, larkspur, rosebuds, straw flowers, statice, sea lavender and lady's mantle.*

LEFT *A lush summer garden filled with a wide variety of flowers and plants will provide many opportunities for the designs.*

which, for maximum impact, you would probably use in clusters – to the sturdiest of hothouse or border flowers, you can create wreaths and garlands with virtually any fresh flowers of your choice. The comparatively recent introduction of absorbent foam – and in this context especially its production in the form of preshaped rings – means that flowers may have a ready source of moisture and the designs have a longer life potential.

Some designs offer no such moisture source for fresh flowers. Examples of these are wreaths created on twisted-twig bases or moss-covered wire frames, and garlands composed around a core of wire or cord. Even so, fresh flowers may be preferred to their dried counterparts, for the short-term, here-today-if-not-tomorrow benefits they offer, and the special effects that can be created for a one-day event or party. In this case, it is more than ever important to treat the fresh plant material carefully as soon as you bring it indoors – the simple process known as conditioning, which is discussed more fully below.

HARVEST TIME

If you have the chance to gather fresh flowers and leaves from a garden, or, with permission, plentiful materials from the wild, then you have the opportunity to condition them when they are at their peak, and they will reward you with optimum longevity. Even the time of day when you harvest materials has a significant effect on both their appearance and life expectancy. Avoid cutting plant materials in the heat of the sun; noon on a summer's day is the worst possible time. This is when flowers and foliage of all kinds are at their most vulnerable and least able to cope with the transition from growing plant to severed design component.

If you are harvesting materials that you intend to dry – lavender to weave into a nostalgic wreath for the bedroom, perhaps, or straw flowers to contribute their simple daisy-like shapes to an "everlasting" wall decoration – then the timing is even more critical. Unwanted moisture on the plant materials hinders the drying process – i.e. the extraction of the natural moisture contained in the petals – and may even completely inhibit it. And so it is advisable to gather flowers for drying after the morning dew has dried at mid-morning and before the evening dew settles damply and irrevocably on them; so, in order to avoid the wilting effect of the noonday sun, this means mid-afternoon. It goes without saying, of course, that rainy and mist-laden days are out of the question for "dried harvesting."

Gathering plant materials at just the right stage of their development calls for another piece of careful timing. If you are planning a one-day design to decorate a festive or party scene, then you will want the flowers to be almost at the peak of their maturity; almost, but not quite. Flowers that are fully developed (cabbagy, full-blown roses are an example) are also on the verge of their downward spiral, in both visual and development terms, and are likely to wilt much more quickly than ones that are harvested a day or so earlier.

When flowers are intended for a longer lasting arrangement (say, for a fresh-flower ring to decorate the table throughout the long Easter weekend), then it is advisable to select flowers which are far from being fully open. In this way you will not only ensure that they "stay the course," but you will have the pleasure of watching them develop gradually from day to day.

Flowers for drying should, in almost every case, be cut at the half-way-to-maturity stage. Roses in tight bud or semibud dry much more successfully than those that have been left to develop on the plant. Slender stems of spike-like flowers (larkspur, clarkia, and the stately delphinium are examples) should be harvested for drying when the topmost flowers are in tight bud, the central ones are just beginning to open and only the lowest ones are fully developed.

Branches of preserved leaves have a highly decorative role to play in wreath and garland designs, from short snippings of frosty green eucalyptus blended with wintry materials in a Christmas table wreath to swathes of copper-gold beech leaves wired with fruit and flowers in the burnished shades of Fall, an eye-catching design for a Thanksgiving or harvest festival celebration.

Gathering deciduous leaves for preserving – a reassuringly simple process described right – requires, once more, sensitive timing. It is important to cut the branches when the leaves are fully mature and while the sap is still rising in the plants. Cut the stems too early in the season, when the leaves are still young and tender (and this limitation applies to evergreens, too), and the foliage is likely to wilt during the preserving process. Cut them too late in their development cycle, when the sap has stopped rising and the leaves are beginning to lose their natural moisture and change color, and they will not be able to take up the preserving solution successfully. That is the bad

news. The good news is that you can harvest branches throughout the summer, processing a few at a time, and build up a collection of russet, bronze and copper-colored leaves to twist, weave and bind into long-lasting decorations around the home or in a church.

THE RIGHT CONDITION

As we have seen, the transition from growing plant to design component represents a quantum leap for both flowers and leaves. To minimize the shock of being severed from their food source, stems must be put into intensive care almost from the moment of harvesting. In effect, this simply means that they must be given a good long drink of water and left in a cool place for several hours – overnight if that is convenient – before being arranged.

When you are harvesting plant materials on a hot and sultry day, it is advisable to take a bucket or bowl of water with you, strip off any leaves that would come below the waterline and place the stems directly into it. This may not have quite the romantic appeal of wandering from plant to plant with a rustic flower basket over your arm, but it will pay dividends in terms of longevity and freshness of appearance. If you plan to gather plant materials in the wild or from a friend's garden some way away, be prepared to wrap the stems in a bundle of damp tissues or a wad of cotton, and – especially in the case of small and delicate wild flowers – enclose them completely in a plastic bag. The condensation that will form inside will become a valuable moisture source and help to keep the flowers fresh throughout the journey.

Flowers that you buy from a florist or market will already have endured one journey since they were harvested, and may well have another before

ABOVE You can have the best of both worlds by combining the aesthetic pleasure of gathering flowers and foliage in a rustic basket with the practical precaution of putting the stems straight into water. A bowl of water in this small willow basket gives instant refreshment to variegated mint, cornflowers, nasturtiums and rose campion.

unpromising-looking specimen. Pick off any discolored outer petals, of roses, for example, until you re-create an unblemished bloom. Snip off torn or insect-damaged leaves from otherwise healthy sprays; any resulting lack of symmetry will be indiscernible in a finished design. And snip off any bare stem ends which may have carried the earliest-flowering blooms. Natural as these are on the plant, barren stems take on a most unattractive appearance in a design.

THE DRYING PROCESS

From an aromatic wreath of, say, purple sage and rosemary leaves, chive flowers and fennel seed heads that will decorate the kitchen throughout the year, to a romantic garland of paper-crisp midsummer flowers to embellish the bride's table at a midwinter wedding, dried plant materials have a versatile and highly decorative part to play in wreath and garland designs.

In some cases – of which the herb wreath is an example – you can create the design with fresh materials and, as long as the conditions are right, simply leave it to dry, to become a long-lasting and delightful reminder of the herb garden on a summer's evening. And this reminder will, for a time at least, be more than just a visual one, as the herbs will retain much of their original and highly evocative aroma.

you get them home. Even if, as a result, they do look a little jaded there is no need to despair. Cut a short piece – about 1 inch – at a sharp angle from the end of each stem and stand them in a deep container of water to revive them. Flowers that have a reputation for drooping (ranunculus, tulips and roses, for example) benefit from being tightly wrapped in newspaper, right around the bunch of stems and up past the flower heads, before being immersed.

Once the flowers and leaves have been revived, take a critical look at each stem – your last chance to do so before you spend time and trouble arranging them or preserving them for later use. Discard any flowers or foliage sprays that are still droopy or wilted; they are beyond recall. Look carefully at the others; it may be that a little cosmetic treatment can rescue many an

In other cases – when, for example, a winter wedding or other special celebration is ringed on the calendar – you can plan to dry all the materials you will need for the occasion. You may have the opportunity to plant a patch of everlasting flowers such as statice, straw flowers, and sea lavender – all of which are remarkably easy to grow from seed and among the simplest to dry after harvest. Or you may choose to buy high-summer flowers from the florist when they are most plentiful and least expensive and dry them for use as the occasion arises. You may receive an especially romantic or touching gift of fresh flowers which you would like to keep as a permanent memento, or, like so many enthusiastic floral designers, you may simply wish to build up a storehouse of preserved materials that you can turn to decorative advantage as the mood takes you.

Whatever the reason, whatever the whim, drying and preserving plant materials is an absorbing and economic facet of floral art. It enables you to capture and appreciate the beauty of your favorite flowers far beyond their natural flowering times, and even to turn the growing seasons head over heels. If the brightest of spring blooms, sunshine-yellow daffodils, say, are top of your popularity list and you wish to include them in designs for a party six months on – well, all things are possible.

The process of drying flowers, seed heads, and certain leaves is encouragingly, almost unbelievably simple. By far the greatest proportion of plant materials may be dried simply by hanging, either in bunches or singly, in a free circulation of air in a warmish room. Other flowers, such as daffodils, with their clearly defined trumpet shapes, are dried in desiccants, in powder or crystals that gradually and gently draw out the natural moisture from the petals, leaving the flowers with all their original and characteristic shape and form.

As we have seen, the best results are obtained by harvesting flowers for drying well before they start to dry on the plant. Seed heads are another matter, and the indoor drying technique may be seen as an extension of the process already begun by the heat of the sun: poppy heads with their chubby, urn-like shapes and wide range of pastel and neutral colors; love-in-a-mist seed heads wrapped in a veil of crisscrossed green strands and often with dramatic purple striping; silver-gray, velvety lupin seedpods, which can be snipped into wing-like pairs; honesty seed heads with their glistening silver, moon-like, papery disks; feathery grasses with seed carriers that sway in the slightest of breezes; and Chinese lantern plants with their vibrant orange hues or, captured at a slightly earlier stage, a contrastingly soft and delicate green

There is a huge variety of plants and flowers that can be easily dried including daffodils (below) and poppy seed heads (left) which are already partially dried from the sun.

coloring. Seed heads offer a whole range of decorative materials that may be considered as a second flowering of the plant. Indeed, many seed carriers have so much design potential that the floral artist and gardener has a tricky decision to make – whether to harvest flowers in their moment of glory, or to leave them to go to seed and undergo their natural design transformation on the plant. A happy compromise, gathering some flowers to use fresh or to dry, and leaving others to be enjoyed when their "second personality" develops, might well be the solution.

Generally speaking, leaves give best results when they are preserved in glycerin, by a simple process described on page 16, or – a technique well known to generations of children – when they are pressed between sheets of absorbent paper and put under a heavy weight. But there are exceptions, and some leaves can be dried successfully just by exposure to air. These include sage and purple sage, rosemary and bay (all perfect candidates for a herb wreath), or Jerusalem sage, lady's mantle, and eucalyptus. The craft of preserving plant materials is frequently one of choices and alternative techniques – there are more ways than one to preserve the beauty of many flowers and foliage types. As an illustration of the point, it is also possible to preserve rosemary, bay, and eucalyptus leaves in glycerin. The method may be slightly more time consuming; the results will be different – the leaves will emerge darker, more supple and glossy – but the choice is there.

LEFT *A collection of materials air-dried by hanging. There is quaking grass, hare's tail grass, silver leaved (white leaf) everlasting and lady's mantle.*

AIR-DRYING

The process of drying plant materials in a warm, airy room, the simplest and most widely used of the techniques, involves nothing more scientific than hanging or standing the materials in a container in a temperature ranging from 50°F to about 90°F. The actual time taken to reduce the materials to the paper-crisp stage of dehydration necessary to prohibit mold growth will vary according to the initial moisture content of the plant, the humidity of the "drying chamber" and, of course, the temperature.

The lower the temperature, the longer the plant material will take to dry. But since hanging bunches of vibrant straw flowers, golden tansy, snow-white baby's-breath, and spiky teasels, to name but a few, are, even in the drying process, a decorative feature, time is not of the essence. You can hang materials on coat hangers on hooks on the wall, on a string line stretched across a room corner, on a hook in an unused chimney recess or alcove – anywhere around the home that offers the requisite dryness of atmosphere.

Poorly ventilated rooms, such as damp carports and garages, and steamy bathrooms and kitchens are not suitable. The material would take up extra moisture faster than it could shed it.

A higher drying temperature, giving speedier results, is best suited to the larger plant materials such as heavy spikes of delphinium, showy peony heads and bunches of rosebuds. Such domestic conditions, which might be produced in a warm cupboard with the door left ajar, are the closest one can get to the drying methods used by professionals, in which flowers are dried in well-ventilated cabinets heated by controlled blasts of hot air.

Hang-drying at room or warm cupboard temperature is suitable for any flowers composed of a mass of tiny flowerets, whether they form umbrella-shaped heads such as yarrow, tansy and achillea, or tight little clusters such as the spectacular and fluffy mimosa, an eye-catching component in a mixed flower wreath or a summery wedding garland. Materials composed of numerous flowerets arranged on long spikes (delphinium, larkspur, clarkia and mullein are examples) may be dried in this way, too. If lack of height becomes a problem – as it may above a boiler or in a cupboard, for example – then these lofty materials may be dried flat, on absorbent paper placed on shelves or racks. In this case they should be turned every day or so, so that the air has access to each surface in turn.

Grasses, too, especially those with a heavy head-to-stem ratio, may be dried flat or standing upright, loosely arranged, in a dry container. Decorative grasses such as hare's-tail grass, quaking grass, and more common meadow types have wide application in country-style designs, as the principal component in midsummer and harvest wreaths, and in Thanksgiving and harvest garlands, and as a decorative and neutral foil to showier materials in other designs. And so, at the height of summer, the message is to take a pair of secateurs and a large flat basket, and to go grass gathering.

Some flowers may be dried by what is known as – a seeming contradiction in terms – the water-drying technique. It is tempting to believe this was discovered by accident, by someone who left a couple of heads of hydrangea, a bunch of creamy-white pearl everlasting, a few veil-like sprays of baby's-breath or a bunch of cornflowers in a little water, forgot to top it up, and then found that the flowers had dried satisfactorily. All you need for this method is about 2 inches of fresh, cold water in a clean container. Leave the stems in a warm room until both the water and the flowers have dried, and the process will be complete.

Dried hydrangeas are particularly valuable for wreath making, so it is a good idea to capture every pale blue, pale pink, and deep wine-red flower head that comes your way. Snipped into clusters of three or four flowerets on adequately strong stemlets, they are ideal to arrange around the inner and outer rims of absorbent foam rings, where they will both conceal the unlovely mechanics and create an attractive background for more expensive or precious materials. Soft, heathery colored blue hydrangea flowerets could be blended to beautiful effect with, say, bright blue dried cornflowers and cream rosebuds to create a blue-for-a-boy christening decoration that would form a permanent memento of a happy occasion.

Cornflowers, whether they are piercing blue, vibrant pink or deep, deep wine-red, are among the most versatile and decorative of materials to dry. See how well they blend, for example, with the medley of herbs in a wreath shown on page 108. Here is a flower that can be successfully dried in a variety of ways: in situ in a wreath created on a moss-covered ring; by hanging in bunches in a warm, airy room; by being left to stand in a little water in a container; and by the thoroughly modern method of preserving plant materials in a microwave. Experiment with different flowers and see how well they preserve.

Microwave drying is far removed from the

BELOW LEFT *Grasses may be dried upright in a container; in this case bulrushes, pampas grass and hogweed.*

BELOW *Hydrangea heads and baby's-breath may be dried by immersing the stems in a small amount of cold water.*

LEFT *Flowers such as cornflowers may be dried effectively in the microwave by arranging them as shown in the picture.*

that can be successfully preserved by air-drying. The microwave method is not suitable for "hollow" or trumpet-shaped flowers (freesias and daffodils, for example), which just collapse.

Preserving plant materials is never an exact science, even in so highly computerized an appliance as a microwave oven. The exact time taken to dry the materials to cornflake crispness will, as always, depend on the volume of moisture they contain, and, of course, the volume being processed. In general terms, however, flowers and small leaf sprays are dried after three to four minutes on full power.

The process is simple. Place a piece of paper towel on the turntable (a fresh piece of paper for each batch) and arrange the plant materials so that each stem is separate. A wheel pattern with stems to the center, flower heads to the outside, is ideal when processing cornflowers. Check the materials after three minutes. If they do not feel and sound paper-crisp, give them a little extra time. Leave them to cool for a minute or so before removing them from the oven and transferring them to a box lined with tissues.

DESICCANT DRYING

The techniques of air- and microwave-drying make it possible to preserve a wide range of plant materials, from towering spires of delphinium and golden rod (which can both be snipped into a multitude of small wreath components) to tight clusters and spheres such as pearl everlasting and mimosa. The use of desiccants, or drying agents, makes it possible to extend this preserved harvest still further and include hollow and trumpet-shaped flowers such as Peruvian lilies, orchids and narcissi; larger composite flowers such as marguerites, spray chrysanthemums and marigolds; more flat-faced examples such as butter-cups, camellias and anemones; and those with tightly clustered petals such as ranunculus and zinnias. By this means you can also preserve fully opened flowers of Canterbury bells, foxgloves and delphiniums – invaluable in wreaths using such a range of deep to delicate blues and mauves – and stems of lily-of-the-valley and grape hyacinth, both romantic and pretty components for wedding and christening designs.

You can use any one of a number of desiccants, or a mixture of more than one; your choice may depend on the number of flowers you plan to dry, and their size and type. Silica gel crystals, which you can buy in drug stores and other specialist stores, are available in two forms, the standard white crystals and the color-indicator type which have a built-in reassurance factor. These crystals, which are sold by

DESICCANT DRYING

1 *A shallow layer of ground silica gel crystals forms a base for cosmos and nasturtium, the first stage in the desiccant drying process.*

2 *The crystals are sprinkled over the flowers to cover them, and then the box is covered with the airtight lid. The flowers should be dry in two or three days.*

traditional country craft of hanging bunches of garden flowers on, say, a wooden airing rack until the petals have yielded all of their natural moisture. But it is a speedy and effective way of preserving plant materials, and one which encourages experimentation. It is suit-able for small composite flowers such as cornflowers, senecio and feverfew; for flat, open-faced ones such as pansies – a truly delightful ingredient in a floral wreath; for snippings of multi-floweredted examples such as lady's mantle and marjoram, and for certain leaves, of which sage, purple sage and silver-leaved "evergreens" claim the highest success rate. As will be clearly seen, all these suggestions apply to materials some florists and flower clubs, are blue when they are dry and turn pink as they absorb moisture. Both types should be ground to a fine powder, using either a mortar and pestle or a food processor. (Wash these thoroughly before using again for food.) Silica gel crystals are the most costly of the drying agents but, like all the others, they can be strained (to remove small dried plant particles), dried on trays in an oven at low temperature, and used over and over again.

Alum powder and household borax powder, both obtainable from some supermarkets, can be used in a half-and-half mixture with silica gel crystals, or with dry, clean silver sand. Sand alone, too heavy to use with small and delicate materials, can be used for large, showy blooms such as mop-head crysanthemums and dahlias, both with brilliant design potential for wintertime garlands and swags.

In this method of preserving plant materials, in which the desiccant replaces air as the drying medium, it is important that every side of every petal or leaf comes into contact with the powder. Sprinkle a thin layer of drying agent to cover the base of an airtight can or box, cut short the stems of materials to be preserved and place them, well apart and in a single layer, on the powder. Sprinkle desiccant over and around the flowers, using a spoon or letting it trickle gradually through your fingers. Do not add a heap of desiccant all in a rush, or you will crush and deform the petals. Use a small camel-hair or similar paint brush to ease the desiccant into the crevices of the flowers and, when you are satisfied that they are all completely covered, sprinkle on a "top coat" of the desiccant. Cover the container with its lid and, if it is not a good fit, seal it with tape. Set the box aside and check the flowers after two or three days. Carefully scrape away the desiccant – the paint brush is useful for this delicate operation, too – and test that the flowers are dry and crisp. If they are not, cover them with the desiccant again and leave them for a further one or two days. When they are ready, brush the flowers to remove any particles of desiccant, and store them between tissues in a box in a warm, dry place. Remember that by now the dried flowers will be brittle and will need careful handling, especially if you need to mount them on wires to extend the length of the stems to fit your arrangement.

PRESERVING IN GLYCERIN

Preserving foliage and certain bracts in a solution of water and glycerin may be seen as the very opposite of the drying techniques. For just as air-drying leaves plant materials, to a varying degree, crisp, brittle, and

with a matt surface, "glycerining" renders materials soft, supple, and shiny. The process is suitable for both deciduous and evergreen foliage, and bracts such as bells of Ireland, hops and hydrangea. Not only that, it can be employed to preserve berries and other fruits on the stem: blackberry stems complete with their glossy jet-black fruits, holly sprays vibrant with red or yellow berries and red cedar sprays heavy with clusters of minute cones.

Long sprays of leaves and stems of bracts are preserved upright, their stem ends standing in about 2 inches of the preserving solution. Short sprays and large individual leaves (some types of ivy, fatsia and fig, for example) may be processed in a flat container, completely immersed in the solution.

To prepare the material for preserving, cut or pick off any damaged leaves and discard them. Cut stems and branches into manageable lengths and split or crush woody stems with, respectively, a sharp knife or a small hammer, to facilitate the intake of the solution. Scrape away bark for about 2 inches from the stem ends for the same reason. Wipe large leaves or any that are dull or dusty with a clean, damp cloth.

Make a solution of two parts of glycerin to three parts of very hot, but not boiling, water and mix it well. Pour the liquid into upright or shallow containers, and stand or immerse the plant materials in it. Leave them for about seven days before checking. When the preserving solution has replaced the natural moisture, leaves should have darkened considerably in color and be glossy and bright. Some may have beads of the solution appearing on the surface.

When they are ready, remove upright stems from the solution, wash and dry them. Wash immersed leaves in soapy water, rinse and dry them. Store

ABOVE *The process of preserving in glycerin is suitable for both deciduous and evergreen foliage, such as firethorne berries and rose hips, fern leaves and bells of Ireland bracts.*

FINISHING TOUCHES

While preserved leaves emerge with a high-gloss and light-catching finish (far shinier, in many cases, than in their original state), berries, hips, and haws tend to lose a little of their characteristic glister in the process. This can easily be restored with a light coat of clear, colorless varnish, an application that has the added advantage of helping to maintain the shape and form of the material: a useful antiwrinkle cosmetic! The same treatment can work very effectively on nuts – pecans, chestnuts, walnuts, almonds – which will shine stunningly in a harvest swag, a Christmas table centerpiece, or a Thanksgiving wreath. Brush the nuts lightly with varnish and leave them to dry before wiring them (see page 32); this way you will avoid the fixing material taking its share of the limelight.

The fluffy, down-like seed carriers of dried **Clematis vitalba**, known as old man's beard, can be "held" with a light spray of hair spray which, without ever revealing its presence, will keep every wayward wisp in place. Remember to spray sparingly because hair spray tends to dull colors. This material, which can be gathered freely in late summer, makes a notable texture contrast with flowers, nuts, and foliage in Fall wreaths and garlands.

Pecans, chestnuts, walnuts and almonds to be used in a harvest swag can be given a highly polished effect with a light coat of clear varnish.

LEFT *Materials most at risk are fresh flowers and leaves arranged with no moisture source and the finished design needs constant attention to prolong its life and attractive looks.*

branches and stems in upright containers away from strong light in a dry, airy room; individual leaves may be stored between tissues in a box. Strain the glycerin solution, which will probably be brown and slightly cloudy, and store it in a stoppered bottle. Reheat it for future use.

Preserved leaves and bracts, glossy with glycerin and with their glowing autumnal hues, are a great addition to wreath and garland designs. Snippings of copper beech contrast attractively with delicate pink flowers like modern pinks and spray carnations in summertime wreaths, and larger sprays can be twisted and woven into shimmering garlands. Hops can be twined around twisted-twig wreaths or used to outline a piece of furniture at harvest or Thanksgiving time, and bells of Ireland, which emerge a deep, rich parchment color, can be cut into single bracts or pairs for inclusion in fresh- or dried-flower wreaths. Evergreen sprays preserved with berries make stunning and long-lasting winter displays. You could, for example, combine short sprays of blackberries and black-berried ivy with contrasting red straw flowers in an "everlasting" wreath for winter. And, for even more of a vibrant color in the preserved leaves, you could add a dye to the glycerin solution.

LOOKING AFTER YOUR DESIGNS

It may be said that there are three stages in the creation of wreaths and garlands: the harvesting and selection of the plant materials; the process of drying or preserving those materials so that they may, if appropri-

ate, be used in long-lasting designs; and the artistic composition of the designs themselves. We hope that the projects described and photographed step-by-step on the following pages will provide you with a plentiful source of inspiration for making wreaths and rings, ribbons and swags to grace every occasion.

Once you have completed a wreath or garland design and step back proudly to admire it, it is time to turn your attention to stage four, the care and maintenance of the design; the attention to detail that can help prolong the life of fresh materials and keep preserved ones looking their best for the longest possible time.

Obviously the materials most at risk are fresh flowers and leaves that have been arranged without a moisture source – freesias and Peruvian lilies inserted in a twig ring to decorate a church at Eastertime; scabiosa, cornflowers and marigolds strung onto a garland to set the scene for a midsummer barn dance; a bridesmaid's headdress fashioned from sweet peas and pinks to be her crowning glory on that special day; a circlet arranged around a stylish hat, an elegant accessory for a summer party outfit.

If the flowers have been well conditioned and given a good, long drink of cool water, they will be off to a good start. As soon as they have been arranged, give them the cool-water treatment again. Spray them with a fine mist spray or a laundry spray, and keep them in a cool place until they need to be put on display. Few of us can emulate the cool room that florists use for this purpose, so we must improvise. A cellar, the stone floor of a north-facing pantry, an airy shed or outhouse, or even the refrigerator are all possibilities. The bridesmaid's headdress shown on page 60 was sprinkled with water, placed on damp tissues on a cookie sheet and kept on the bottom shelf of a refrigerator until the photographer was ready to take the final picture! Likewise, the wire circlet composing the straw-hat decoration on page 79 can be kept in a cool place until the last minute, and fixed around the hat just before leaving for the party.

Even fresh flowers that have been arranged in a moisture source, such as any inserted in an absorbent foam ring, benefit from the refreshing effect of a mist spray at least once a day, more often in hot and sultry weather. Remember to remove the decoration from a non-water-repellent surface, such as a wooden table top, before launching forth with a flurry of water; and remember to keep the absorbent foam permanently moist by carefully pouring water around the surface of the foam. A characteristic of such foam is that once it has been allowed to dry out, it will not reabsorb moisture, completely losing its efficacy, and its ability to keep fresh flowers looking fresh.

BELOW *After the flowers have been arranged, spray them with a fine spray or a laundry spray, and keep them in a cool place until they need to be put on display.*

However, do not spray fresh-flower and foliage designs that are to be left to dry in situ; they will be more likely to falter instead of drying attractively and almost imperceptibly. And take care when mist-spraying the flowers on a paper-core garland such as the one shown on page 75. Cover the exposed areas of twisted paper with a piece of plastic so that the water spray does not reach it and weaken it.

If one or two flowers in a design start to wilt ahead of the others, remove them, or pick off the discolored petals so that they do not become the focus of unwanted attention in an otherwise pleasing display. If you do not have a reserve of replacement flowers, fill in any gaps with a spray of foliage – after giving it a reviving drink of water – or slightly readjust other materials in the design to cover the traces.

No matter how diligently you condition and spray fresh flowers that are arranged without a moisture source, their display days, unfortunately, are numbered. If you have created a design for a single day or a party – and you can bear to dismantle it the morning after – it is an act of sensible frugality to rescue the flowers, put them in water, and rearrange them so that you can enjoy them for several days to come. No matter how short the stems, you can assemble a medley of flowers – freesias, pinks and spray carnations from an Easter candle design, perhaps – in an absorbent foam ring where they will live happily not-quite-ever-after.

The joy of dried-flower arranging is completely different. You know that the time and trouble you take in creating each design, whether it is a heart-shaped rosebud wreath as a Valentine token, or a blue and cream circlet to celebrate a christening, are investments for the future. It is true that most dried flowers will eventually fade, but they have an indisputable charm even in this advanced stage of maturity.

To give dried-flower designs the best possible chance of retaining their colorful personalities – the deep sky-blue of larkspur, the dazzling pink of peony, the brilliant yellow of tansy – the golden rule is to position them well away from strong and direct sunlight.

Reserve the sunniest hot-spots for wreaths made of materials already bleached and matured by the sun – a hoop of wheat, oats or barley; a ring of dried grasses or some wheat bunches, nuts, and cinnamon sticks.

On long-lasting designs, a film of dust will eventually play its part in obscuring the original color of the plant materials, and add to what is sometimes called their "faded charm." The simplest remedy is to take the design to an open window and give it a "good blow" or a few blasts of air from a hair drier.

ABOVE *If a design has been created for a special occasion or a single day, the flowers can be rescued and reassembled in a more casual manner where they can live happily for several days.*

RIGHT *Placing the design in direct contact with the wind is one way to clean it if it has collected any dust.*

CHAPTER 2

COLOR AND STYLE

Whenever you are planning to make a wreath or garland in celebration of a festival or special family occasion, or a floral decoration to enhance your home, your first consideration will almost certainly be the color of the plant materials you use, which, more than any other aspect of the design, will give the decoration its individuality, personality, and style.

Some occasions and events are traditionally associated with one or more colors, and these will help to guide you (although they should never be allowed to restrict you) in your choice of fresh and preserved materials. Yellow, blue, and white are the colors that have special significance at Eastertime; but, just for the joy of it, we chose to blend them with soft pastel pink flowers in our Easter-table, candle, and wall decorations. And how pretty and seasonal they look! By contrast, the inspiration for the Greek *stefani* ring to decorate a cottage door on May Day (see page 44) is drawn from all the myriad colors of a flowery meadow. And so, in this essentially pastoral wreath, anything, in terms of color, goes.

ABOVE AND LEFT
Color is a crucial aspect to any design and certain decisions must be made right at the start, such as whether it will be multi- or single-colored.

THE COLOR WHEEL

To make color work the way you want it to in your wreath and garland designs, it is a good idea to make a quick "ready reckoner" of the color spectrum, known as a color wheel. Draw a rough circle, divide it into six segments, and color or write the names of the three primary colors – red, yellow, and blue – in alternate spaces. Color the three secondary colors in the blank segments, orange – a mixture of red and yellow – between those colors, then green, and lastly violet. Then you have only to glance at the wheels to see which color partnerships or trios will give you the boldest or most subdued effects.

A ring of lime-green lady's mantle and cornflowers, for example, would be an unusual but reasonably restrained floral combination for a midsummer party decoration, since green and blue are neighbors on the color wheel. But add a dash of red – which is opposite green and next-but-one to blue on the wheel – and you have a stunning color blend. Add the red ingredient in the form of luscious strawberries, and your guests will be drooling!

The combination of red and blue, both strong primary colors when they are used at full strength – in deep shades – can be striking, even elegant, as it is in the decoration of roses and cornflowers ringed around the garden-party hat (see page 79).

For a much softer and younger-looking expression of these colors, select flowers in the pastel tints, pink and palest blue, as we have done for the circlet of sweet peas and spray carnations shown on page 54.

Wheel 1: *Primary and secondary colors; Tints and Tones*

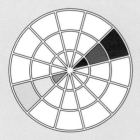

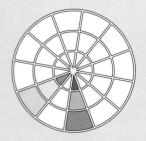

Wheel 2: *Complementary colors*   **Wheel 3:** *Harmonious colors*

Much the same may be said for designs to decorate a midsummer fete, barn dance or party – designs that we have brought together in a chapter called Midsummer Night's Dream. At this time of year, if the sky is deep, deep blue and the sun a burnished gold, floral decorations have to be brighter than bright to compete or even to be noticed. This is the time for eye-catching blends of orange and blue, and yellow and purple, accentuated with complementary flashes of white. And if the weather does not come up to expectations – well, there is nothing like a brilliant splash of floral color to set the party scene.

Designs created at harvest and Thanksgiving time – the wreaths and garlands that decorate our churches and other places of worship, homes, and party venues – take their color cue, and their materials, too, from the golden cereal crops, the copper-bronze of the falling leaves and the fiery hues of showy seasonal flowers such as dahlias and chrysanthemums. Lest such designs should blend too perfectly with their surroundings and seem like camouflage, it is a good idea to add sharp accents of scarlet and brilliant green, in either flowers or ribbons.

Red and green are the traditional colors of Christmas decorations, represented by the berry-bright evergreens that ancient peoples brought indoors for their then supposed magical powers. Swathes of glossy or matt-surfaced foliage are a perfect foil for all that glitters – for varnished nuts, gold- and silver-sprayed seed heads such as poppy, small seasonal fruits, and the zingiest of dried flowers, straw flowers

especially. But the color brightness should not come only from the accessories. Try to select evergreens that make a color statement, too. Variegated holly and ivy speckled from the deepest green to clearest yellow, branches of silver-green and frosty looking fir, lime-green cypress, blue-green juniper, and spotted laurel are a far cry from the monotonous shades of dark green that were once fashionable.

As it happens (and it can surely be no more than a coincidence) the traditional blend of green leaves and red berries, baubles and bows that typifies Christmas decorations is an example of one of the color combinations guaranteed to create a dramatic effect. This is because the two colors, furthest apart from each other on the colour spectrum, exemplify the attraction of opposites. Other color combinations which are next to each other on the spectrum – orange and yellow, or green and blue for example – are considered more harmonious and, in spite of their individual brightness, have a less dramatic effect.

THE RIGHT BACKGROUND

The color of the background has a significant effect on the way a design is "read," too, on whether it is perceived as a real eye-catcher or more of an understatement. Place a blue and white decoration – our nostalgic dried-flower ring around a Parianware pitcher (page 104) for example – against a green wallcovering and the effect, created by two neighboring colors,

RIGHT *When dried flowers are arranged using bunches or clusters of the dried materials rather than single units, the design will have a far more pronounced color impact. As many as 10 or 15 can be bunched together to form sizeable highlights.*

would be pleasingly modest. Transfer the group to a position where it would be seen against an orange curtain on the other hand (blue and orange being opposing colors on the wheel), it would take on a vastly different and even brash personality.

Backgrounds have such a profound influence on the overall effect of a design, not only in terms of color, but in texture, too, that they should be brought into consideration at the very earliest planning stages. If you are asked to create designs for a church festival, to decorate a public hall for a function, or to set the floral scene for a party, it is well worth making a site visit at the outset. Measure the wall, altar or windowsill you are to decorate, and take a piece of cord or string to simulate the rise and fall of a garland or swag. Take a note of the color and texture of the wall or backdrop, and the amount of light the area receives. All these details will help you to design decorations that will be shown to their full advantage.

If you wish to create a floral wreath in pale peaches-and-cream tones, for example, it would be a good choice for a dimly lit area, but might not be clearly seen against a pale stone wall. In such a case it would be a good idea to outline the wreath with a ring of dark, glossy leaves: ivy, sprays of box and bay, or laurel would all make a suitable frame to highlight the principal ingredients, the pastel colors.

You might, as another example, plan to compose a wreath to be shown against the intrusive background of a heavily pointed red brick wall. The contrasting colors and strong geometric pattern created by pale mortar and dark brick present fierce competition for a delicate design. This situation calls for a bold approach: an evergreen wreath with large clusters of pale-to-mid-tone flowers would hold its own visually. Pinpricks of small flowers on the other hand, would give it a spotted and insignificant appearance.

BELOW AND OPPOSITE
Backgrounds have a profound influence on the effect of a design; the same wreath set against different colors and textures can alter the character from casual and rustic (below) to rich and sophisticated (opposite).

ADDED COLOR

With every color in the rainbow represented in the whole wonderful world of fresh and dried flowers, it is reasonable to take the view that you cannot improve on nature. But there are instances when the addition of nearly natural or sheer fun colors can extend your range of plant materials in an interesting and enlivening way. Take seed heads, for example. Most of them have varied and fascinating shapes, yet few of them make a generous contribution to a design in color terms. Sometimes the neutral tones of creamy beige poppy heads, say, can be a welcome foil to other, more colorful materials such as jewel-bright dried peonies. But there are occasions (Christmas is one) when those seed heads would be the perfect design accessory, if only they were red.

Take sea lavender, a plant that dries into multi-flowered spikes which are virtually everlasting and immensely versatile, but not very colorful. Snippings of the stems, in all their wayward directions, make pretty, ragged outlines to a dried-flower wreath, give a dainty summery look to a dried-flower garland, and contrast effectively with round and spherical flowers of all kinds. If your stock of sea lavender is uniformly pearly white, as much of it is, buy a specialist nontoxic flower spray paint, spread out the dried plant on ample sheets of newspaper and color it pink, blue, yellow or the shade of your choice.

And, just for fun, take honesty, an invaluable plant for bringing a dash of natural glint and glitter to Christmas and party decorations. Add a few sprays of the silvery disks to brighten evergreen wreaths and garlands; make a bright-as-a-beacon wreath of tightly packed honesty sprays alone, or add a few snippings to catch the light in designs composed of matt-surfaced flowers. But there is no need to leave it there. Retain the natural gloss but add a nearly neutral color, such as pale green or pale pink, by spatter-spraying the seed disks. It's honesty with a most attractive difference.

LEAF COLOR

The technique of preserving leaves in a glycerin solution (see page 16) has a natural coloring effect, darkening the tissues until laurel leaves emerge nearly black, eucalyptus turns deep gun-metal blue, rosemary and bay take on an even deeper shade of green, and beech becomes dark chestnut brown. Since the range of color in preserved materials is somewhat limited and, admittedly, not always particularly attractive, it is interesting to experiment by adding a little commercial dye to the glycerin solution. In this

way the plant material takes up, not only the preserving agent, but color, too, and it is possible to obtain some fascinating effects. Try adding green dye when preserving beech, oak, maple, and chestnut leaves, ivy, rhododendron, choisya (if available), and ferns. The depth and brightness of the resultant color makes the leaves a pleasing choice for natural-looking and long-lasting garlands, and an interesting alternative to the use of familiar evergreens.

For more "authentic" autumnal tints, you can add red dye to the preserving solution for eucalyptus leaves, which become copper-bronze, and to copper beech, which takes on a cheerful fieriness. Lime bracts, which make useful components in long-lasting wreaths, take well to a rust-colored dye.

ABOVE *Seedheads such as teasels have fascinating shapes but their neutral tones can be a bit dull. Placing them with colorful peonies for example, can enhance them a lot.*

CHAPTER 3

MAKING THE BASES

From a luxuriant circlet of brilliant midsummer flowers to a hoop of sun-bleached oats; a ribbon of trailing leaves and fresh or dried flowers edging a celebration table, to a paper garland strung with herbaceous blooms to set the scene for a party – the beauty, elegance, and style of wreaths and garlands of all kinds is determined by the base or core on which each design is constructed.

Decorations of this kind have been made for centuries in countries all around the world from the simplest and most natural materials. Children sitting in a grassy meadow would pick daisies and make a chain by slotting each stem into a slit made in the one before, others twisted around a handful of supple stems such as grasses, cereal stems, or willow, into a hoop, bound them with twigs or twine and decorated the ring with posies. These posies might have been made of the brightest wild flowers around – a May Day tradition in the Greek countryside, where the colorful rings were, and still are, hung on cottage doors; or of dried grasses, their modest and neutral shades accentuated by the addition of a few brilliant flowers – a charming tradition from the Provençal region of France, where young girls would wear these floral rings in their hair. Other wreaths would be bound with glossy, glowing evergreens and brought indoors to decorate the homes in wintertime. It is the continuation of this ancient ritual which has become part of our own Christmas tradition.

In the joyous spur-of-the-moment spirit of the occasion, it is still possible, and remarkably simple, to make wreath and garland bases from the natural materials all around us; bases which, if they show in the final design, are at one with the decorative materials used. You can considerably extend the range of design possibilities by using other materials, techniques and products that will enable you to use a wide variety of decorative materials in imaginative ways and – an important consideration – to keep fresh flowers in the peak of condition for several days.

BELOW *A selection of wreaths, rings and bases you are able to buy or make. From bottom left, clockwise, green twisted stem wreath; twisted-twig ring; absorbent ring; bleached willow wreath.*

NATURAL STEM WREATHS

In keeping with tradition you can first make a circlet, or a wreath base, from practically any supple stems. The actual ones you choose will depend, as it has always done, on local availability and their suitability. You can make a circlet from the most delicate of grass stems – as we have done for the design for the grass posy ring in Chapter 6, which can be decorated with equally light and flimsy materials such as bunches of grass, dainty wild flowers, or delicate dried flowers. Going up the strength scale, it is advisable to use slightly more sturdy stems (bryony, perhaps, or the tips of weeping willow) to support more weighty decorations such as posies of heavy headed flowers, and thicker stems still (they could be clematis, vine, honeysuckle, or wisteria) for a wreath to support sturdy cones and generous posies of woody evergreens.

As many of our flower designs will show, your choice of wreath base need not be a matter of practicalities alone. Many circlets made of twisted twigs, with their attractive variety of natural features, are decorative items in themselves, and need be only partially covered by the floral or leaf decoration.

To make the simplest of natural bases, take a handful of long grass stems and divide them in half. Reverse one half of the stems and place them, tip to base, on top of the others to even out the thickness. The purist, and certainly our rural ancestors, would use grasses to bind the stems, but it is easier to use raffia, thin string or garden twine, all of which are less inclined to split, unravel or in any other way demonstrate their independence. Take the twine around one end of the grasses and knot it to secure it in place. Bind over and around the stems as evenly as you can, gathering them up neatly as you do so. Slightly overlap the two ends, bind them together and take the binding a little further on to be on the safe side. Knot the twine around the ring, cut off the end and neaten up the ring by cutting off any stray and wayward wisps.

The base of the Greek *stefani* ring on page 44 is made in a similar way from bryony stems. Other possibilities for a "middleweight" base of this kind are the supple green stems of Queen Anne's lace or any other wayside umbellierous plants. Later in the season when the stems have dried they are less flexible, and need to be soaked in water before they can be used in this way.

Once you have bound a strip of grasses or other slender stems, you can vary the way you use them. As a variation on the traditional circlet, for example, you can shape the bound stems into a figure of eight, binding them both where they join and where they cross in the center, or into a lover's knot. To make this romantic design, twist the strip of bound stems into an oval-shaped loop with the ends not joined, but crossing over to branch off into a V, then simply bind the stems where they cross. For another hint of romance, you can form the stems into a heart shape – a pretty outline for a Valentine, engagement, or wedding gift. To do this, it is necessary to cheat a little, and conceal a preshaped piece of thick wire among the stems. To extend the design potential still further, you can use a strip of bound stems as a natural and supple core for a light floral garland to drape over a doorway, hang beneath a windowsill, or over a fireplace. As you overlap and bind in more and more bunches of stems there is no limit to the length of core you can make.

Nimble fingers can shape a strong and heavy-duty circlet from stout, but always supple, tree, hedge, or shrub cuttings without recourse to any other fixing materials. You simply gather up a handful of twigs (actinidia, birch and willow can be added to the examples already given) entwine the first two, one around the other, bend them into a circle and entwine others to link them and strengthen the core. Usually eight to 10 twigs will give the dimensions needed. Then, to give the circlet stability, bind it around and around with one or more twigs of the same kind, a "self-binding" that becomes part of the design. Even the hook to hang a wall decoration can come from the same natural source – a twisted twig loop whose ends are woven securely in and out of one side of the ring.

Another and perhaps simpler way of making a sturdy twig ring is to shape the first twig into as near a circle as possible, slightly overlap the two ends and bind them with thick roll wire. Then twist and turn each additional twig over and around the first one, winding in more pieces until you have the thickness you require. If the twig base is to be completely covered by the additional decorative material, then there is no reason (except perhaps the purely aesthetic one) why you should not bind the ring with, preferably, brown twine. If part of it is to show, as it will if you intend to bind on just a few delicate dried-flower posies at widely spaced intervals, then for appearance sake it is best to bind and secure the ring with more twigs.

For anyone who does not have access to a handful or so of supple twigs, or does not have the aptitude to twist and turn them into decorative wreath shapes, there is a wide range of bases now available from florists' stores, floral art clubs and department stores. You can buy twisted-twig bases in all sizes and made from a wide variety of materials: smooth chunky ones from stout and shiny brown willow twigs, or parchment-colored bleached willow; rugged rings of

MAKING A TWISTED-TWIG RING

You can make a twisted-twig ring of the kind shown here, in many of our designs.

YOU WILL NEED

---

roll of wire

scissors

secateurs

supply of twigs, such as clematis, wisteria, birch, willow, vine, or honeysuckle

---

1 Cut the twigs to equal lengths. Bend one twig into a circle, slightly overlapping the ends. Bind the stem ends with roll wire. Wrap a second twig around the first one, then a third twig around those and so on.

2 When the twig ring is the thickness you require, take a slender and supple twig, insert it between those in the ring and wrap it around them to bind them. Secure the end of the binding twig and insert another one if necessary to complete the binding. Cut away the wire that held the first twig.

3 The finished base, which can be used in a wide variety of designs, such as the Easter wallhanging described in Chapter 4.

knobbly vine; lover's knot and heart-shaped ones to inspire romantic floral designs; and thick country-style rings of tightly packed stems covered with a decorative top layer of dried grasses.

SHAPING UP WITH WIRE

Using natural or purchased materials for making wreath and circlet bases and the core for garlands and ribbons, gives rise to special satisfaction derived no doubt from the centuries-old traditions. But it could be equally satisfying to create delightful decorations with bases made of other materials.

Wire of all types and thicknesses is readily available and easy to use. A wire coat hanger from the dry cleaners, with or without its original hanging hook, can be reshaped into a circle or heart and serve as the hidden base for a wall decoration emblazoned with fresh- or dried-flower posies, bunches of herbs and evergreens, or a parade of cones. A piece of thick wire cut from a roll can be shaped into a circlet and bound with the prettiest of flowers, sweet peas and spray carnations, for example, to create a bridal head-dress. Or, cut to just the right size to fit tightly around the brim, it can be wired with flamboyant ribbons and flowers to bedeck a garden-party hat. Stub wires, which you can buy from florists, can be shaped singly or two-in-a-row to form a circle with similar applications. And plastic-covered electrical wire has just the right flexibility to form a flower garland for a child to wear at a festival.

If there is a chance that the secret bit of mundane wire base might be revealed, it may be preferable to bind the core first with raffia, gutta-percha tape, or, for special-occasion designs, narrow ribbon. The tape, available from florists in a variety of colors, sticks to itself as it is bound, each twist slightly overlapping the one before. The copper-wire wreath frames you can also buy from florists are infinitely adaptable and inexpensive. There are two types, each usually available in at least two sizes, with a diameter of 10 inches and 12 inches respectively. One is the "flat" type, formed of two concentric and level rings joined together by soldered wire strips. An example of this type of frame can be seen in Chapter 7, where it is bound with brown gutta-percha tape, and then with dried oats to make a light-filtering, sun-streaking window hanging. The other frame type is "dished," with the inner ring set at a lower level than the top one. This second type, which has built-in depth, is particularly suitable for covering with dry sphagnum moss or with hay as the basis for an evergreen wreath or a dried-flower circlet. Covered in this way, with a textured and highly evocative natural material, the wreath base need not be filled in its entirety. As the peony ring described in Chapter 8 shows, an area of planned exposure – of hay in this instance – adds immeasurably to the charm of the design.

For more substantial wreaths – a design in which you might want to fix large, heavy cones or pieces of fruit – you can construct a base of wire mesh rolled around sphagnum moss or hay or, for water retention, small blocks of absorbent foam. Similar materials can be used in similar ways to form the core for garlands and floral ribbons. Thick wire, bound with gutta-percha tape, will hold any angle you require of it, even a straight, horizontal line, while a thinner wire will take more readily to the gentle curves and arcs often associated with designs draped across the front of a party table. Again, it is important to take suitability into account. Thin wire will sag unevenly under the weight of heavy decorations.

Rope, cord and string of all kinds are other suitable materials for garland bases. On page 38 we show you how to conceal a core of this type with a wrapping of dry moss or hay. This way you obviate the show-through problem which so often occurs when wired-on bunches of the decorative materials (it may be holly and ivy for a Christmas garland) twist down and hang, albeit horizontally, beneath the core rather than against it. Here again, a glimpse of moss or hay can even enhance a design, and will certainly not detract from it.

Other suitable core materials for garlands include braided raffia – which also makes an effective and chunky base for a swag (see page 84), braided straw, and twisted paper ribbon. You can use the tightly rolled paper for a lightweight garland core as we have done in the design on page 75, opening it out at intervals for an interesting textural contrast. The fully opened paper strip is used to decorate bows for an integrated finishing touch. However, it is as well to listen to the weather forecast before planning paper garlands as outdoor decorations, as they do not take kindly to rain!

At the other extreme, in terms of weight capacity and endurance, is a garland core made in a similar way to a wreath base, from wire mesh rolled around moss, hay, or blocks of absorbent foam, and then covered with moss or hay. Cores of this kind are the most expensive and time-consuming to construct, although they can be stripped and stored for reuse. Also, you will find that the finished design was worth the extra effort. You might choose this method for a Thanksgiving garland composed of bunches of wheat, heads of Indian corn, globe artichokes, squashes and other vegetables which would prove too weighty for wire or string.

PREFORMED SHAPES

The comparatively recent introduction of plastic foam as a floral art material has opened up new design horizons, and has greatly increased the potential "shelf life" of decorations made with fresh flowers. There are two types of florists' foam, sold under various brand names. One absorbent type, usually green, is for using with fresh flowers and foliage; the other type, which may be gray or brown and has a slightly sparkly finish, is for use exclusively with dried flowers. Both types are available in blocks slightly larger than a building brick, which can be cut to any shape; in cylinders about 2¼ inches deep and 3 inches across (which we used to form floral "torches" in Chapter 6) and in preformed rings up to 10 inches in diameter.

If you can buy these ready-made rings from your florist or floral art club, you will find them inspirational in the composition of table-top and wall-hanging designs of all kinds. If you cannot obtain them you can cut absorbent or dry foam blocks to form a circular shape to hold fresh or dried materials. In Chapter 4, Spring Festivals, we show you how to create an Easter table centerpiece from foam strips arranged around a large, flat plate; and in Chapter 7 there is a dry foam ring cut from a block of gray foam to outline a candlestick. Another option is to use a china or glass

FINISHING TOUCHES

To make a hook for hanging a wreath, you can use stub wire. Bend the wire to make a circular shape in the center and twist the two ends beneath it. Push the wire ends through the outer ring of the frame and bend them back to secure.

When you are creating a wreath to be used as a wall decoration, you need to plan the hanging device to be in keeping with the mood and style of the design.

Some ready-made twisted-twig rings that you can buy already have a hook, perfectly in tune with the ring itself, made of a similar twig woven into the circular structure. When making your own wreath of twisted twigs, you can follow this traditional practice.

To hang wreaths made of a moss- or hay-covered wire frame, of bound grass stems, or of a preformed dry foam ring you can make a hook from a stub wire and attach it firmly to the frame. If the hook shows, it is preferable to cover the wire in a "sympathetic" material. This might be raffia, gutta-percha tape, ribbon, or dry grass. To keep grass firmly in place and prevent it from uncoiling, it is usually necessary to bind it at the beginning and end with a few twists of fine roll wire. When you have bound the stub wire with the appropriate material, make a round loop in the center and firmly twist the two wires beneath it. Insert the two free ends into the back of the wire ring and twist them around the frame, or push them from the back to the front of a dry foam ring, bend them upward at the front of the foam and press them close against the surface. The wire will then be concealed by the flowers.

MAKING A MOSS OR HAY WREATH

You can cover a wire ring with dry sphagnum moss or hay to create a good-looking, country-style wreath base.

1 *Tie the wire or twine to the outer ring of the frame. Take a handful of the moss (which is shown in the photograph) or hay and wrap it around the back and front of the ring. Bind it over and over with the twine, pulling the binding tightly so that it is buried deep in the covering material.*

2 *Add more moss or hay and bind it on all around the ring until the frame is completely covered.*

3 *The ring frame covered with moss can now be used as a natural-looking base for decorations of evergreens, dried flowers, and herbs. The decorative materials should be wired and the wires pushed through the moss to the back of the frame and secured there.*

ABOVE *Wires are used to support decorative materials such as cones, nuts and fruit (in this example, apples) which have inadequate stems or no stems at all.*

posy ring, or a ring-shaped metal cake pan, and fill it with small blocks of foam arranged to fill the circle. Small gaps between the blocks are inconsequential, and will be covered by the leaves and flowers.

When cutting absorbent foam blocks to make outline shapes it is best to cut the material dry, and then to soak only the pieces you need for the design. Store the offcuts dry, for future use. You may want to use them, for example, to fill a wreath or garland core made from rolled chicken wire. Soak absorbent foam blocks or rings in cold water until they are completely saturated, and keep them permanently moist. Once the foam dries out it will never reabsorb moisture to its original capacity. For this reason, you must store used absorbent foam in sealed plastic bags to prevent it from drying out. Then just give it a quick soak in water before using it again.

None of the complimentary descriptions that have been accorded to twisted-twig rings and wire frames covered with sweet-smelling hay can be applied to absorbent or dry foam rings. They are strictly practical design aids and distinctly unlovely to look at. This means that you must plan your designs so that every scrap of the foam surface and the green waterproof casing of absorbent foam rings will be out of sight.

As you will see from our step-by-step designs, the way to do this economically, and without using too many precious flowers, is to outline the ring with plentiful or inexpensive materials. You could press short sprays of, for example, ivy leaves, snippings of box, clusters of lady's mantle, sea lavender, or hydrangea flowerets, close against the foam to mask it, and then fill in the design, and partially cover the outline material, with the feature flowers. Another way, which is especially suitable for a rustic design with mid-summer or Fall overtones, is to cover the ring with moss or hay held in place by staples of bent stub wires. The way to achieve this complete cover-up is shown on page 34. For a design with the festive spirit, when a surfeit of ribbons is in order, you can wrap a piece of toning ribbon, the prettiest of masking tapes, around the base of the foam ring. We have done this in the Advent candle design in Chapter 9.

You may cover soaked absorbent foam rings with the prettiest of summer flowers, such as sweet peas, roses and veil-like baby's-breath, to decorate the tables at a wedding reception, or with a stunning medley of roses, nasturtiums and pansies to trail from the rustic basket. You may stud a dry foam ring with dainty dried flowers in pink or blue, and present it to the parents at a christening, or use one to make a floral ring around a favorite ornament. Our design for a circlet in Chapter 8 pays a pretty compliment to a simple pitcher. Whatever design you choose, the holding material must, in cases like these, be very much behind the scenes.

WIRING TECHNIQUES

Wires of various kinds have an important, although largely unseen, part to play in many wreath and garland designs. Firstly, wire of varying thickness can be used as the core material for circlets and garlands, in designs ranging from a bridal headdress to a herbal ring. Wires are used to support decorative materials such as cones, nuts and fruits, which have inadequate stems or no stems at all; to provide false stems for flower heads, which have become detached from their natural ones; and to bind flowers and foliage sprays into posies. Lastly, wire (usually roll wire) is used to attach decorative materials to wreath and garland bases.

The most useful wires for your floral tool kit are stub wires and fine silver roll wire. Stub wires are available in several thicknesses, from fine through medium to heavy gauge, and in lengths from 3½ to 18 inches. Two or three types will be sufficient; there is certainly no need to invest in the whole range. Heavy-gauge stub wires can be used to wire large and weighty pieces of fruit such as apples and oranges. The technique is shown in a stage photograph for the Halloween ring in Chapter 7. Medium-gauge wires may be used to wire small-to-medium-sized pine cones, nuts, and poppy seed heads – when the natural stem is too thick to pierce the holding material and stay firmly in place. These wires may be used, too, to bind bunches of woody stemmed material such as evergreens, and to make hooks for hanging wall decorations.

Fine silver binding wire, which is similar to fuse wire, is used to bind fresh- and dried-flower posies, and to attach these and other materials to a garland core. A useful tip when using this wire is to place the roll in a cup to prevent it from rolling off the table and getting tangled. But there are times when it is easier to cut off a working piece of wire from the roll and add in another piece as it is needed. Useful, even invaluable, as it is in the creation of wreath and garland designs, wire is not a decorative material and should, whenever possible, be completely concealed. For this reason garlands and swags are usually designed so that the tip of one posy covers the bound-on stems of the previous one all along the line. In other cases, a design may include ribbons entwined around the ring or garland in such a way that they form a decorative, colorful, and purposeful camouflage to the basic mechanics, and nobody would be the wiser.

COVERING A GARLAND CORD

When you want to make a decorative swag or garland of heavy materials such as twigs, evergreens, or fruits, rope or thick cord are the most suitable materials for the core. To avoid any problems of "show-through" and to give the core a natural look, you can cover it with dry hay or sphagnum moss.

YOU WILL NEED

———

piece of rope or thick cord

twine, or you can use a roll of fine silver wire, for binding dry hay or sphagnum moss

scissors

———

1 Measure the piece of cord or rope you will need. Allow for gentle drapes in the way the garland will hang. Tie the twine or wire close to one end of the rope. Take a handful of hay, wrap it around the rope and bind it over and over with the twine. Pull the binding tightly so it is almost concealed within the depth of the hay.

2 Continue to wrap the rope with hay, and bind it for the length of core you require.

3 Once you have a hay- or moss-covered core, you can decorate it with a variety of materials. Here, mixed bunches of evergreens – holly, ivy, box and juniper – are bound on with green twine.

COVERING A FOAM RING

*P*ractical but by no means pretty is an apt description of both absorbent and dry foam rings. One way to effect a complete disguise is to cover them with dry hay or sphagnum moss before adding the decorative materials.

YOU WILL NEED

---

absorbent or dry foam ring

stub wires

dry hay or sphagnum moss

wire cutters

1 *Even before you begin the disguising process you can see what a great transformation is afoot.*

2 *Cut stub wires in half and bend each one over to make a U-shaped staple. Place handfuls of hay (shown in the photograph) or moss on the foam ring and secure with the staples. Work all around the ring until it is completely covered on the top and both sides.*

3 *You can decorate a dry foam ring or an absorbent foam ring with any dried materials that have firm, sturdy stems — peonies, sea lavender, statice, roses, cereals, and many more. Those with slender or insecure stems (straw flowers are in this category) will have to be wired.*

The Projects

CHAPTER 4

SPRING FESTIVALS

Since earliest times, the arrival of spring and the rebirth of nature has been celebrated with flowers. Flower festivals were held in many parts of the world, and people decorated their homes and places of worship with colorful wreaths and garlands.
The Easter festival of the Christian church, regarded by many as the most important in the religious calendar, may fall at any time between late March and the end of April, its date being calculated according to the phases of the moon.
Flowers in blue, white, and yellow, among the prettiest that spring has to offer, have come to symbolize the rebirth of Jesus Christ, and are used in church decorations.
The celebration of May Day, a very old tradition strongly linked to those early festivals of flowers, is still enjoyed in many rural areas with processions of children wearing floral garlands and headdresses and carrying simple posies. The tradition of dancing around the Maypole persists in some regions, and in Greece, a floral wreath is still hung on the doors as a symbol of good luck.
Our springtime designs capture the mood of both the religious and the pastoral festivals, from a candlelit centerpiece for the Easter table and altar candles ringed with flowers, to a wall decoration displayed in chapel or church; from a dazzling door wreath of wild and cultivated flowers to a daisy-chain garland that a child might wear for a parade or a party. Spring has always been a time to celebrate with flowers.

EASTER WALLHANGING

Two twisted-twig rings joined together in a figure of eight are an unusual feature of this spring-time wall decoration, which would look effective in a chapel or church.

YOU WILL NEED

2 twisted-twig rings of
different sizes

stub wires

wire cutters

flower scissors

pink and green satin
ribbons, ¾-inch wide

scissors

slender, supple leaf stems,
such as weeping willow

Peruvian lilies

freesias

1 *The two twisted-twig rings we used were 9 inches and 6 inches in diameter respectively, but similar in thickness. The flowers and leaves have been well conditioned for several hours in cold water.*

2 *Bind the two twig rings together with stub wires taken around and around. Check that they are held securely, and tuck in the wire ends at the back.*

3 *Push the ends of the leaf stems under the twig binding, and carefully pull them through so the stems outline the circular shape of the rings. It does not matter if some of the stem tips are not secured at this stage.*

4 Cut stub wires in half and bend them to make U-shaped staples. Cut short stems of the flowers and place them, singly or in pairs, on top of the rings. Secure the flower stems, and any wayward tips of the leaf stems, with the wire staples, pressing the ends between the twigs.

5 Bind one piece of the ribbon around the lower ring, taking it over the flower stems to conceal the wire staples. Secure the ends at the back of the design.

6 Wind the second color of ribbon around the top ring in a similar way, and finish it with a bow at the top. Spray the flowers with cool water.

GREEK MAY DAY RING

Capture the joy of the Greek springtime festival, *protomayia*, by making a colorful flower ring, known as a *stefani*, for the front door.

YOU WILL NEED

supple stems, such as bryony, weeping willow, or Queen Anne's lace

raffia or twine

scissors

flower scissors

selection of brightly colored fresh wild and cultivated flowers, such as poppies, cornflowers, marigolds, spray chrysanthemums, marguerites, feverfew, sweet peas, and nasturtiums

1 Simplicity is the keynote of these traditional country-style rings which are made with natural materials. A handful of bryony stems, supple in springtime, forms the core of the wreath. You can choose raffia or green twine both to bind the core and to bind on the flowers. As the flowers will have no moisture source, give them a good long drink of cold water before commencing the design.

2 Gather the stems neatly and form them into a tightly packed strip. Secure the binding material at one end and bind it around and around the stems, pulling it tightly as you do so. Any leaves still attached to the stems are bound in, and just add to the informality. Overlap the stem ends slightly, and bind them together. Ease the core to make a neat circular shape.

3 Bind on small flowers in mixed bunches, large ones singly or in pairs. Do not try to even out the colors or balance the flower shapes around the ring. The charm of designs of this kind is their air of spontaneity.

4 Continue binding on more flowers around the ring, the heads of one cluster covering the stems of the previous one. If a little of the ring base shows in the finished design it will not in any way detract from the pastoral effect.

5 *When you have completed the ring, spray the flowers with a fine mist of cool water, and repeat this several times a day, especially in hot weather. In Greece the flower rings are left on the doors for several weeks, and they gradually fade.*

CANDLE GARLANDS

Plain white candles are transformed into the prettiest of Easter decorations with a ring of pastel flowers and trailing ribbons.

YOU WILL NEED

plain white candles; ours were 12 inches long and 1 inch in diameter

roll of fine silver wire

scissors

flower scissors

short pieces of satin ribbon, ¾-inch wide

freesias

Peruvian lilies

spray carnations

spray chrysanthemums

baby's-breath

1 We chose plain white "altar" candles, but you could decorate small white household candles, or ones in various colors, in a similar way. As you need only a few flowers, you could use snippings left over from larger designs, making the garlands to match a table centerpiece or wall decoration.

2 Bind the silver wire around the candle and secure it. Place a few flowers on the candle and bind the stems with the wire. Position more flowers close to the first ones, and bind the wire around the stems to secure them. Continue until the candle is encircled by flowers, and secure the wire.

3 Bind the ribbon once around the candle to cover the wire, and tie it in a double knot, leaving the ends trailing. Cut the ends on a slant to neaten them.

4 *The finished candle garlands. Spray the flowers with cool water to keep them fresh. They can look equally good on a dining table or a sideboard table.*

DAISY CHAIN

*T*his simple garland of daisy-like spray chrysanthemums for a child to wear at a May Day festival has sentimental echoes of the daisy chains of our childhood.

YOU WILL NEED

flexible cord or plastic-covered
electrical wire

strong adhesive tape, such as
insulating tape

scissors

roll of fine silver wire

flower scissors

slender, supple leaf stems, such
as weeping willow

spray chrysanthemums

HINT

Spray chrysanthemums are a good choice for a design that will have no moisture source and may be worn for several hours of celebrations. Give the flowers a good long drink of cool water before arranging them, and spray them with a fine mist of cool water at intervals. If you have to compose the garland in advance of the occasion, you can keep it fresh for several hours in the refrigerator.

1 Use flexible cord or insulated wire to form the core of the garland. This electrical wire is covered in white plastic. If not, you could bind it first with white gutta-percha tape before binding on the leaves and flowers. Butt the two ends of the wire together and bind them with insulating tape.

2 Place one of the foliage stems close to the wire core and bind it securely with roll wire. Cut short the stems of chrysanthemums. Place one over the leaf stem and wire, and bind it securely. Position another flower with the head to cover the stem of the first one, and continue around the garland.

3 Reverse the direction of the flower heads at the center of the garland by criss-crossing the stems of two flowers and binding them to the core. Make sure that the "opposing" flowers are close enough together to conceal their stems.

4 *Tuck in extra stems of leaves to fill out the design and to help cover the wire core. For the prettiest effect, have some leaves trailing on both the inside and the outside of the garland.*

5 *Our daisy chain was designed in two colors, with only the white flowers worn against the brilliantly colored embroidery of the festival dress. The different flower color at the center back and front adds interest to the composition.*

EASTER TABLE RING

*F*lickering tapers and a "nest" of eggs set the scene for this pretty Easter table centerpiece.

YOU WILL NEED

large flat plate

small shallow dish

block of absorbent foam

knife

string

scissors

moss

flower scissors

6 thin candles

eggs

variegated leaves, such as periwinkle

freesias

spray carnations

Peruvian lilies

HINT

This is a quick-and-easy way to make a foam circle when you do not have, or cannot obtain, a preformed foam ring. You can use a block of dry foam in a similar way to make a dried-flower table ring.

1 The making a ring of absorbent foam (slices cut from a dry block) – a flat plate to form the base of the design, and a shallow dish to hold the moss and eggs.

2 Cut the foam block into slices 1¼ inches wide. Cut each slice in half across the width, and trim off the top and bottom corners.

3 Soak the foam pieces in water for several minutes. Arrange them around the plate and tie a piece of string around the outside of the foam blocks to hold them in place. Put a handful of moss in the dish.

4 Start building up the design by positioning short sprays of the foliage around the inner and outer rims of the foam circle, so the leaves overlap the edges. Cut short the stems of the Peruvian lilies and position them to face inward and outward.

6 Fill the design with spray carnations, their stems cut short and the flower heads resting close against the foam. Arrange the brightest flowers, in this case the yellow freesias, at intervals. Check that there are no gaps in the design and that no foam shows through at all.

5 Turn the plate around, complete the ring with one color of Peruvian lilies, then add the second color. Again, face the flowers alternate ways, with some overlapping the rims of the plate and dish.

7 Cut each candle into two pieces of uneven lengths. Use the knife to scrape away the wax from the top of each of the lower pieces, to expose a short piece of the wick. Press the candles into the foam to form a cluster at one end of the design.

8 *Arrange a few eggs on the moss in the center of the floral ring. These could, if you wish, be painted or dyed. Have some more candles ready to replace the first batch as they burn down, watch that they do not burn too close to the flowers.*

CHAPTER 5

WEDDINGS AND BAPTISMS

*Of all the most joyful and momentous occasions in our lives,
weddings and baptisms are perhaps the ones
when family and friends most ardently want to express their love and
affection with flowers. These are the occasions
too, as they have been for generations, when we want every location –
the church or chapel, public hall, house and
garden – to be looking most festive. And that means being garlanded
with flowers!
Our suggestions include two delightful designs for a bride or her
attendants to carry and wear. Both are items
that the bride's mother or a close friend could easily create with pride
and affection. The headdress, a simple circlet
composed on a wire frame, could be echoed in the flower arrangements
to decorate the wedding tables; our designs
include a "floral wedding ring" that would make the prettiest of
table centerpieces.
Then there are the tables themselves. When all eyes are on the
celebration cake or the bride's table, or guests
are invited to help themselves to a buffet or to drinks, the table has a
high, decorative profile. Our ideas include a
garland of dried flowers to bring a hint of summer to a party table at
any time of the year, and beribboned swags to
drape prettily across the fall of the tablecloth. This garland and
swag, so effective and yet so simple to make,
have other applications, too. You could make one to wind around the
pillars in a church, across the altar or
along the stage in a public hall, to decorate a windowsill or an arch, or
to outline a door. The location may be totally
different, but the method and its effect would be similar.
To celebrate the birth or baptism of a child, an
occasion when admiring friends and relations want to "say it with
flowers," we have a dried-flower posy ring
that can be made in moments, and treasured as a lasting and loving
memento.*

FLORAL WEDDING RING

Created in colors to blend with those worn by the bridal party, this flower ring could decorate the table in the vestry, or the bride's table at the wedding reception. The addition of baby's-breath creates a veil-like effect which is especially suited to the occasion.

YOU WILL NEED

---

absorbent foam ring, 10 inches in diameter

floral scissors

sprays of light evergreen leaves, such as box

spray chrysanthemums

roses

modern pinks

sweet peas

baby's-breath

1 Place the flowers and foliage in cool water before arranging them. This will help to prolong their freshness. Soak the absorbent foam ring in water for several minutes until it is completely saturated.

2 Cut short the evergreen sprays and arrange them around the inner and outer rims of the foam ring, trailing downward so they mask the base. Position other sprays around the top of the ring, where they will alternate with the flowers and give a natural look to the design.

3 Cut short the stems of spray chrysanthemums and position them, some facing inward and some outward, around the ring. You can use the flower buds, too, to give variety of size and shape.

4 Place the roses, the largest of the flowers used, at equal intervals around the ring. Fill in the design with pinks and sweet peas, balancing the colors more or less equally. Turn the ring around and check that there are no gaps and that the foam and base are completely concealed. If not, add a few more sprays of foliage or flowers.

5 Cut sprays of baby's-breath and trim off any wayward stems. Position the sprays around the ring so they come just above the other flowers and partially obscure them, like a veil. Spray the flowers with a fine mist of cool water.

6 This floral wedding ring, created in pastel tints of pink and blue, would be a pretty decoration for a summer wedding. To tone with other bridal color schemes, it could be composed of peach-colored roses, apricot-colored sweet peas and cream spray carnations, or yellow roses, blue cornflowers and cream spray chrysanthemums.

FLORAL TABLE SWAG

Whether it's a wedding in a rented hall, a christening party in the garden, or some other special family celebration, a floral swag draws flattering attention to the table and sets the scene for a memorable occasion. This one is composed, somewhat unusually, of asparagus fern, variegated mint, and hollyhock flowers.

YOU WILL NEED

———

thick string

roll of fine silver wire

scissors

flower scissors

white-headed pins

ribbon, 1 inch wide

asparagus fern, or another "feathery" foliage such as maidenhair fern

variegated mint or another variegated foliage such as periwinkle

hollyhock flowers; or you could use roses or mallow

———

1 *The delicate effect of this swag is achieved by using light-looking foliage and flowers – feathery and variegated leaves and pale-colored flowers with an attractive trumpet shape. For an occasion like this, solid, dark green foliage could make the design look too wintry. If you pick separate hollyhock flowers from several plants, to avoid cutting whole stems, float them in a shallow bowl of water.*

2 *Measure the string to give a gentle curve across the table front. Each side of the table will be decorated with a separate swag. Place one stem each of asparagus fern and mint over the string close to one end and bind it in place by taking the roll wire over and around the stems and string two or three times. Bind the foliage stems all the way along and bind on a hollyhock flower at intervals.*

3 *Bind on more foliage, the asparagus fern and mint together, to make a continuous line. Trim off any particularly wayward pieces (of the fern especially) that would spoil the line of the swag. Fasten off the wire by tying it close to the end of the string. Make further swags in a similar way for each side of the table, reversing the direction the flowers face on alternate swags.*

4 Tie the ribbon close to one end of the swag and bind it around and around between the flowers and over the foliage stems. Do not pull it too tightly; it looks prettier in soft folds. Tie the ribbon close to the other end of the swag.

5 The gentle fall of the swag in close-up. Crisp white cotton is the perfect and traditional backing, although the design would look equally effective on a pastel-colored cloth.

6 Tie the free ends of the string together, and pin the swags to each corner of the table, slightly adjusting the length if necessary to make sure that the drape is even. Make four ribbon bows and pin one to each corner, to hide the joins and make a pretty focal point.

BIRTHDAY GIFT

To celebrate the birth of a baby or a young child's baptism, it is a delightful idea to make a long-lasting floral wreath from dried flowers as a gift for the parents. It will be a charming memento of a proud family occasion.

YOU WILL NEED

twisted-twig ring; ours was 12 inches in diameter

decorative ribbon, ½ inch wide

scissors

flower scissors

roll of fine silver wire

dried straw flowers

dried larkspur

dried lady's mantle

dried baby's-breath

dried rosebuds

dried cornflowers

1 The blue-for-a-boy ribbon has a small polka-dot design. Among the toning blue flowers are larkspur, cornflowers, and dyed baby's-breath. To contrast with them are lemon-yellow straw flowers, greeny-yellow lady's mantle, and cream rosebuds.

2 Form the dried flowers into five posies, each one with a rosebud at the center and a cornflower as a colorful highlight. Arrange the flimsy material to fan out at the top of each posy, to give a full, but dainty looking shape. Bind the dried flower stems with roll wire, leaving a long end, and trim the stems neatly.

3 Leaving one long end to tie into the bow at the top, thread the ribbon loosely in and out of the twig ring, occasionally but not always taking it around and over the ring. Ease the ribbon so that it forms loose loops around the ring. Tie the two ends into a bow at the top.

4 *Place one of the posies on top of the ring. Thread the end of the roll wire through two or three of the twigs, take it over and over several times, and tie it in to secure. Tie on the other posies at equal intervals around the ring. Ease the ribbon loops over the posy stems to conceal them.*

5 *The completed ring, decorated with delicate ribbon and dainty dried-flower posies, can be used as a wall or table decoration in a nursery or living room.*

BRIDAL HEADDRESS

*T*here's a special pride in composing a bridal headdress for a member of your family or for a friend. This simple style, a circlet of sweet peas and spray carnations, would be charming both for a young bride and her bridesmaids.

YOU WILL NEED

2 stub wires or piece of medium-gauge wire

white gutta-percha tape

scissors

roll of fine silver wire

flower scissors

velvet ribbon, 1 inch wide

sweet peas

spray carnations

baby's-breath

HINT

For an attractive and coordinated look, you could use similar flowers and an identical color scheme to make floral-ring decorations for the guests' and bridal tables.

1 Flowers for a bridal headdress are chosen in colors to complement the bridesmaids' dresses and the overall color scheme of the wedding – in this case pink and cream. You can use similar flowers to tone with a mauve and blue, red and white, or blue and yellow theme. Stand the flowers in water.

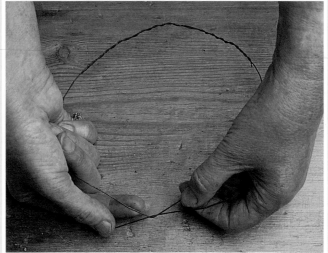

2 To make a circlet from stub wires, twist the ends of two wires together, bend them into a circle, and twist the other two ends together. Or you can make the core from a single piece of wire. For a circlet 7 inches in diameter you will need a piece of wire 22 inches long.

3 Bind the wire circle with gutta-percha tape, slightly overlapping each binding with the one before. Make small, short-stemmed posies of mixed flowers, including a few sweet peas, a spray carnation and a spray or two of baby's-breath. Bind the stems with roll wire and trim the stem ends.

4 Place one end of the posies against the wire circlet and bind it on by taking the roll wire around and around the wire and stems. Without breaking off the roll wire, bind on the next posy so that the flowers cover the stems of the one before. Work around the ring in this way, leaving a small gap for the ribbon bow.

5 Velvet ribbon has an especially luxurious look and holds its shape well. Tie the ribbon around the circlet, tie a bow and arrange it to follow the lines of the ring. Trim the ribbon ends neatly.

6 Spray the headdress with a fine mist of cool water, and keep it in a cool place (even the refrigerator) until the moment it is needed.

BRIDESMAID'S HOOP

Inspired by the dainty hoops carried by the bridesmaids at the Duchess of York's wedding, our design is composed of mainly yellow and white flowers with pretty entwined ribbons.

YOU WILL NEED

piece of bent cane to form a hoop

strong adhesive tape, such as insulating tape

white gutta-percha tape or narrow ribbon for binding

scissors

roll of fine silver wire

flower scissors

ribbon, ¾ inch wide

Peruvian lilies

spray chrysanthemums

spray carnations

freesias

1 Bent cane is an ideal material to make a carrying hoop. We made a hoop 16 inches in diameter from a cane 56 inches long. The flowers we chose are especially longlasting, and therefore well suited to being without a moisture source.

2 Join the two ends of the cane by butting them together and binding them together with strong adhesive tape. Cover the cane circle with gutta-percha tape or with narrow ribbon. While the tape stays firmly in place, ribbon does not. Pull it tightly at every turn to get a neat, even finish.

3 Leaving one long end at the top of the bow, wind the ribbon loosely around the hoop so it forms decorative curves. Tie the two ends into a bow and trim the ends by cutting them across diagonally.

4 *Divide the flowers into twelve groups of different types and colors. With the roll wire, bind one group to the cane so the flower heads wrap around it. Reverse the stems of the next group, position them over the others, and bind them in place.*

HINT

It may be more convenient for you to make the design to a part-way stage and assemble it just before the wedding. To do this, bind the cane hoop and bind on the ribbon, to the end of Step 3. Divide the flowers into twelve groups and bind the stems of each group with roll wire to make a posy. Stand the posies in water until you are ready to complete the design. Then unwire each posy in turn, so that the flowers can be arranged to wrap around the cane and bind them in place.

5 *Bind on more groups of flowers, always in pairs so that the stems overlap and are concealed by the flower heads. Tie the ribbon bow at the base of the design, over the cane and the stems of two flower groups, and trim the ends. Spray the flowers with a fine mist of cool water.*

6 *All ready, complete with dainty lace gloves, for the young bridesmaid to carry. When a design is in two main colors, it can be interesting and effective to add small amounts of a third shade — in this case, the pink of the Peruvian lilies.*

SUMMERY TABLE GARLAND

Whenever there's a special celebration in the family, highlight the party table, whether it holds the drinks, the buffet food, or the cake, with a dried-flower garland. There are twin advantages to using preserved flowers. You can achieve a summery look even in the depths of winter, and you can create the garland well in advance of the occasion.

YOU WILL NEED

thick string

roll of fine silver wire

scissors

flower scissors

white-headed pins

ribbon, 1 inch wide

dried sea lavender

dried statice

dried straw flowers

dried rosebuds

dried peonies

1 *Make your selection of dried flowers in colors to suit the occasion. As only short-stemmed flowers are needed, you may be able to use left over clippings from other designs, or flowers with broken stems. Measure the string, which forms the core of the garland, to go around the circumference or perimeter of the table, then cut it slightly longer, to allow for tying.*

2 *Cut short sprays of the sea lavender, which forms a continuous line along the garland. Tie the silver wire close to one end of the string, bind on a few sprays of sea lavender, and then more sprays to cover the stems. Bind on the feature flowers at intervals until the garland is long enough to go around the table rim.*

HINT

If you are making a garland for a large table, such as a wedding buffet, you might find it easier to make the floral ribbon in two or more pieces, joining them together and making the ribbon bows to conceal the joins.

3 *Pin one end of the garland to the tablecloth, and pin it at intervals all the way around. Tie the two free ends of the string. Make large double ribbon bows, trim the ends and pin them in place around the table, positioning one to hide the join in the string.*

CHAPTER 6

MIDSUMMER NIGHT'S DREAM

The height of summer is the time for impromptu parties and eating out of doors, for the brightest of colors and the barest of workloads. It's a time to set the scene with the freshest and newest decorative ideas around, and to create stunning effects in a matter of moments. A time, in fact, to take a close look at our designs and see how they could fit into your midsummer night's dream!

There's a long tradition in many parts of the world of capturing the joy of the season by making a grass or flower ring to wear in the hair or to decorate the home. Our designs include two interpretations of this just-for-the-joy-of-it design concept: a grass-covered stem ring studded with brilliant pink, daisy-like xeranthemums, charmingly known as immortelles in France, and a circlet composed of grass bunches decorated with scarlet poppies or, again, multi-colored straw flowers.

For a more formal, elegant hat decoration, there's a cornflower and roses circlet to ring an otherwise ordinary straw hat.

In an ideal world, garden or patio parties would perhaps be held against a backdrop of stunning herbaceous blooms. Since most of our party locations are somewhat less exotic, designs such as the three that follow can help to add a touch of glamour. There's a floral garland highlighted by huge paper bows to festoon an outside wall or gate, an idea for plant-them-anywhere floral torches to impart powerful flower color just where you need it, and a basket of roses, a portable feast of midsummer flowers to decorate an outdoor party scene. And for the party table, we have reserved the most eye-catching decoration of all, a ring of flowers and delectable fruits of the season – strawberries. It's an idea your guests won't be able to resist!

STRAWBERRY FAIR

When you are planning the table decorations for a summer party, let your imagination run riot! There is no need to confine your designs to flowers alone – luscious soft fruits can be used to most delectable effect.

YOU WILL NEED

---

absorbent foam ring; ours was 12 inches in diameter

flower scissors

wooden cocktail sticks

lady's mantle

cornflowers

strawberries, about 12 ounces

1 Soak the foam ring in water for several minutes, until it is completely saturated. As an alternative, you could make a ring of foam slices arranged around a plate, as described in the Easter table ring project, and fill the dish in the center with more strawberries.

2 Look over the strawberries, and put aside any blemished ones which would detract from the look of the design. Cut short stems of lady's mantle and arrange them, with a few of the leaves, around the ring, to cover not only the top but the inner and outer rims as well.

3 Complete the covering of the ring with the base material, the yellowy green and fluffy sprays of the lady's mantle which form a soft background to the more showy materials. Arrange cornflowers all around the ring, not forgetting the inner and outer rims.

4 Spear the base of each strawberry with a cocktail stick. By attaching the fruit in this way, with new wooden sticks, it is not harmed, and can be safely eaten when the design is dismantled.

5 *Arrange the strawberries evenly around the ring so their stems rise just above the level of the lady's mantle. Check that no traces of the foam ring can be seen, and fill in any gaps with more flower or leaf sprays.*

6 *With the deep, clear blue of the cornflowers and the scarlet red of the strawberries in place, the vibrant effect achieved by combining two primary colors can be clearly seen. Play up to this bold, bright look by displaying the decoration on a strong matching color such as a dark blue or brilliant red cloth.*

SUMMER DAISY RING

*E*verlasting straw flowers with their simple daisy shapes and brilliant colors are among the prettiest and brightest of summer flowers. You can create a daisy ring on the spur of the moment, when the flowers are fresh, and leave them to dry on the decoration, when it will become a lasting reminder of summer's haziest days.

YOU WILL NEED

decorative grass-covered stem
ring; ours was 10 inches in
diameter

stub wires

wire cutters

flower scissors

ribbon, ½ inch wide

straw flowers
(see Step 1)

1 You may be able to buy a grass-covered stem ring decorative enough to show through the flower heads. If not, you can make one from supple stems covered with a top layer of dried grasses and bound with twine. You may be able to buy the straw flowers loose in a bag from a florist more cheaply than buying them in bunches, on the stem.

2 Cut the stub wires into 2½-inch pieces and bend a hook at one end. Push the wire through the flower center from the top and draw it through, to bury the hook in the middle of the flower. It is a good idea to prepare several flowers in this way before beginning the design.

3 Push the wire into the stem ring at an angle, so the flower head rests flat on the base. Space the flowers evenly around the ring, alternating deep and pale colors, just as they grow. Position flowers around the inner and outer rims of the ring to give it a well-covered look.

4 *Cut four short and uneven pieces of ribbon, varying from 8 inches to 14 inches long, and cut the ends on a slant to neaten them. Bend half a stub wire into a hook and twist it around the center of the ribbons. Push the wire into the inner rim of the ring so that the ribbons hang in the center.*

5 *The daisy ring, with its pretty air of informality, is a delightful decoration to hang on a bedroom door, over a chair or bedpost, or even outdoors, to brighten the setting for a garden party.*

FLOWER TORCHES

When you're giving a mid-summer night's dream of a party, here's the brightest decorative idea around. It's a pair of un-believably simple-to-make floral torches, which can decorate the garden, the patio, the porch, con-servatory, wherever appropriate. You can "plant" the canes in a flower bed, in pots and tubs, any-where you want to introduce some color and create a sensation.

YOU WILL NEED

---

for each torch:

bamboo cane, about 42 inches long

4 cylinders of absorbent foam

stub wires

flower scissors
strips of different colored paper ribbon

selection of long-lasting flowers in white and bright colors, such as feverfew, cornflowers, single roses, rose campion, santolina (silver leaves)

1 Mark the center of each of the foam cylinders to ensure that you position them centrally on the cane. Soak the cylinders in water for several minutes until they are completely saturated. Working over a waterproof surface, push each cylinder in turn onto the cane.

2 The top cylinder should be level with the top of the cane. Bind a stub wire around the cane to keep them from slipping. Cut the stems of the flowers short and to equal lengths. Position the first row of flowers around the base of the lowest foam cylinder, keeping the flowers close together.

3 Continue making the rings of flowers all the way up the foam. Small examples, such as feverfew (shown here) may be gathered into bunches and several stems inserted together.

4 With rings and rings of flowers in red, white, blue, and yellow covering the foam, finish off the design with something of a floral flourish on top. You could use a spray of single roses, a dome of feverfew, the stems cut to graduated lengths, however you like.

5 Gather up streamers of paper ribbon in different colors and wrap them around the cane, just below the foam. Fix them in place by wrapping a stub wire around the cane. The lowest ring of flowers will conceal the wire.

6 You can "plant" the torches in a nearly-all-green part of the garden, in a flower bed, in pots and tubs, anywhere you want to introduce some color and create a sensation.

*The finished flower torches
can also be positioned on
either side of a porch,
doorway or outside
staircase.*

OUTDOOR PARTY GARLAND

*I*t may be a fund-raising barn dance, an informal get-together in the garden or on the patio, or a teenage birthday party. Whatever the occasion, you can brighten the venue by introducing flowers where there were none. Make our floral ribbon garland to hang beneath a windowsill, across a garden gate or from tree to tree in a midsummer gesture that says "welcome."

YOU WILL NEED

coiled paper ribbon

pencil

scissors

roll of fine silver wire

flower scissors

nails or thumbtacks for fixing

selection of long-lasting flowers in white and bright colors, such as spray chrysanthemums, cornflowers, scabious, marigolds, feverfew

1 *Choose the color of the coiled paper ribbon, which forms the core of the garland, to contrast well with the background and to complement the flowers. A pale color shows to advantage against a black weatherboarded wall. A dark color would have more impact on a white gate. Revive the flowers in cool water.*

2 *Open out the paper ribbon at intervals where the coil will not be covered with flowers. It is not only more economical in the use of flowers to leave gaps in the garland, but it also gives the design a built-in change of texture. First, measure the required length of the garland, work out where the gaps will be, and mark the areas on the paper coil, then gently ease out the paper between the pencil marks.*

3 *Divide the flowers into two groups, so each end of the garland matches the other. Gather the flowers into small mixed bunches, and wire them on to the paper core. Wire each successive bunch so the flower heads cover the stems of the one before. The paper bows will cover the stems of the bunches on the ends of the garland.*

4 *Open out enough of the coiled paper to make two large ribbon bows. For a really full and generous look, allow about 1 yard for each. Tie the paper to make a bow in the usual way, and cut the ends on a slant to neaten them.*

5 *Fix the garland in place with nails or thumbtacks and pin a bow at each end. In hot weather, if you spray the flowers with water, protect the paper core and bows from the mist. And if the guests have to retreat indoors in a summer shower, don't forget the garland also needs cover!*

PROVENÇAL GRASS RING

*I*t's a charming Provencal custom for young girls to make rings of dried grasses, decorate them with wild flowers and wear them in their hair at midsummer festivals. Such decorations are so delightful that it is tempting to make one as a decoration if not for the hair then for the home. Because wild poppies have such a fleeting decorative life once they are picked, we show a long-lasting alternative, a grass ring emblazoned with the most colorful of everlasting flowers, straw flowers in zingy red, pink, yellow and orange.

YOU WILL NEED

twine

roll of fine silver wire

scissors

flower scissors

safety matches

long-stemmed supple grasses to make the core

a selection of grasses of varying types, to give as much visual variety as possible

wild poppies or fresh or dried straw flowers

1 *Take a handful of grasses and trim the root ends. Divide the grasses in two, placing the heads of one group over the root ends of the other. Tie the twine close to one end and bind it over and over them all along the length. Bring the other end around to form a circle and slightly overlap the first. Bind over the join and tie the twine.*

2 *Cut the decorative grasses into short lengths, about 4½ inches long. Divide them into colorful bunches. The most attractive effect is achieved when the grasses range from dark brown through pale beige to pastel green. Bind the stems of each bunch with roll wire.*

3 *Place one of the grass bunches flat against the ring and bind it securely in position, using roll wire or twine. Place each successive bunch close to the one before, so that the grass heads cover the stems of the previous bunch.*

4 To give the wild poppies the best chance of a prolonged decorative life, put them in water (even if it is stream or river water) as soon as they are picked. Burn the stem end of each flower for a few seconds by holding it under the flame of a match. Then put the flowers in water again for as long as the impromptu nature of the design allows.

5 Push the stems of the poppies deep into the grass bunches.

As an alternative, attach straw flowers around the ring. To do this, push the flower stems through the strands binding the bunches of grass. With its brilliantly colored floral decoration, the grass ring makes maximum impact when displayed against an all-the-colors-of-the-rainbow background.

GARDEN PARTY HAT

*D*ecorate a simple straw boater with a ring of fresh flowers and it becomes the most chic hat at the party. We chose a striking red, white, and blue color scheme for sheer elegance.

YOU WILL NEED

plain, wide-brimmed hat

piece of thick wire to encircle the brim

wire cutters

ribbon, 1 inch wide

scissors

roll of fine silver wire

flower scissors

stub wire

roses and rosebuds

rose campion

cornflowers

1 Put the flowers in water until you need to arrange them. Cut the thick wire to fit tightly around the hat brim, and make a hook and eye in the ends. This will enable you to fit the finished circlet over the brim without damaging the flowers.

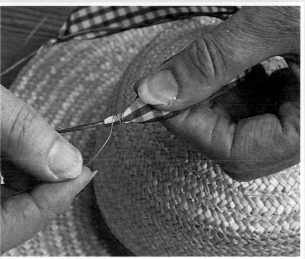

2 Cut a piece of ribbon to fit around the front of the hat and half-way around the sides. Turn one end under, and bind the ribbon to the wire circle with roll wire. Bind the other end in a similar way.

3 Use the roll wire to bind the flowers to the wire circlet. Position the first ones (in this case rose campion) so they cover the bound-on end of the ribbon, alternating the colors. Cut off the roll wire and neaten the stem ends. Wire flowers in a similar order onto the other side of the circlet.

4 Spray the flowers with a fine mist of cool water, using a florist's spray or a laundry sprinkler. Keep the circlet in a cool place (the refrigerator is ideal) until it is time to leave for the party. Make a ribbon bow, ready to fix at the back.

5 Just before leaving, slip the circlet over the hat brim and ease the ribbon at the front so that it lies flat. Bend half a stub wire into a hook shape, push it through the loop at the back of the bow and fix it to the hook and eye on the circlet. Ease the bow so that it lies flat and covers the flower stems.

6 An elegant hat which can be worn for a variety of events.

BASKET OF ROSES

You can make a ring of roses, pansies, and other midsummer flowers to cascade over the sides of a rustic basket, a pretty country-style decoration for a fireplace, patio, or porch. It's a way of making a few flowers look like a million dollars!

YOU WILL NEED

---

round, shallow basket

absorbent foam ring; ours was 10 inches in diameter

flower scissors

trails of greenery, such as variegated mint or periwinkle

roses

nasturtiums

pansies

marjoram flowers

1 *Check that the foam ring fits neatly inside the rim of the basket. Put the leaves and flowers in water before arranging them in the foam. Soak the foam ring in water for several minutes until it is completely saturated.*

2 *Position the sprays of leaves in the foam ring with short lengths to cover the inner rim and longer stems to trail over the outer one. Place the foam ring in the basket again to check that the leaves will cascade attractively. For a casual look, position the stems close to the top of the foam.*

3 *Position the roses, the largest of the flowers in the design, around the ring, with some close to the inside and some toward the outside of the ring. Alternate the colors, pale and deep pink, evenly.*

4 *Fill in the design, grouping several nasturtiums and cornflowers together to create maximum impact. It may be necessary to push a hole in the foam, using a match or stub wire, to position the slender stems of the pansies. Fill in the gaps with short pieces of marjoram, a plant that allows all the others to take the limelight. Place the ring in the basket again, and check that the foam is completely covered. The basket should look full to overflowing with midsummer glory!*

CHAPTER 7

HALLOWEEN, THANKSGIVING AND HARVEST

*As the leaves fall from the trees in a carpet of russet and gold, there is
a seasonal spate of festivals. Halloween,
celebrated on the evening before All Hallows' Day (November 1), has
been observed since earliest times, and has
preserved its spooky associations. This is the night when witches,
demons, ghosts, goblins, and evil spirits were
thought to roam, and people lit bonfires to keep them at bay.
One of our designs, a spiky ring emblazoned with
rosy apples and photographed in a suitably spooky window, was
created in the spirit of the apple-bobbing game,
and could well be hung above the cauldron of floating apples. The
other, focusing on the candlelight so essential to
the mysterious atmosphere of Halloween, is a spiky dried-flower ring
to highlight a table design.
Next is Thanksgiving, the traditional family orientated harvest
festival, celebrated in churches and homes
originally in gratitude for bountiful crops. Those same crops yield a
wealth of decorative materials to make wreaths
and garlands to add to the occasion and other harvest festivals. Sheaves
of wheat and barley form the centerpiece for many
a still-life group in churches, and garlands of wheat and oats may be
strung across the altar or draped to outline a window.
Our designs, deriving from this generations-old decorative
tradition, include a ring of oats which could be
hung in a church window or against a heavy oak door; it looks equally
good in a small cottage window, too. Our harvest
sheaf, composed on a thick raffia braid would be quite a talking point,
hanging on a pillar or post, or duplicated and
arranged on either side of the altar or a door.*

HARVEST SHEAF

As the last of the cereal crops were gathered in, farmworkers used to weave decorative items as a symbol of continuing prosperity on the land. Our harvest sheaf, composed on a raffia braid, is a tribute to that tradition. You could hang it on a door, a pillar or a post, or make a matching pair to outline a window, doorway or an arch.

YOU WILL NEED

thick raffia braid

stub wires

wire cutters

flower scissors

raffia

scissors

ribbons, ¾ inch wide and 1 inch wide

selection of cereals and seed heads, such as wheat, oats, grasses, linseed, and poppy

nuts, such as pecans, hazelnuts, and almonds

cinnamon sticks

dried carthamus flowers or strawflowers

1 You can buy or make a thick raffia braid, which is used as the base of the design. Ours was 24 inches long, 2 inches wide and almost 1 inch thick. Make your selection of cereals, grasses, and other seed heads with an eye to texture and color variety.

2 Prepare the materials for the design. Cut a stub wire in half, wrap it around the center of a nut and twist the ends at the back. You can, if you wish, tie them with raffia. Wrap half a stub wire around the stem of a large poppy seedhead, extending the stem to make it easier to fix.

3 Make mixed bunches of the cereals, grasses, and seed heads by binding the stems with a stub wire and leaving a long end free, as a false stem. Build up the design by pushing the wired materials firmly into the raffia, and group the nuts, cinnamon sticks, and dried flowers in the center, leaving planned open spaces.

4 *Make bows with the narrower ribbon, bend half a stub wire to make a U-shaped staple, and push it through the loop at the back of the bow. Push the wire into the braid to fix the bows as an integral part of the design. Make a bow from the wider ribbon and fix it to the top of the braid.*

5 *The texture and color of the materials, and the different ways in which they attract the light, change throughout the design. Whether you hang it as a wall decoration or display it on an occasional table, the harvest sheaf will be a delightful reminder of the golden days of the season.*

HALLOWEEN HOOP

*I*f you're giving a party for Halloween, and especially if teenagers have a hand in the arrangements, you will want an eye-catching decoration verging on the outrageous. Our apple-and-twig ring comes into just that category, and can be made by even the least adept members of the family.

YOU WILL NEED

twisted-twig ring; ours was 12 inches in diameter

secateurs

stub wires

wire cutters

knobbly, gnarled twigs, such as from an apple tree

apples; we used two varieties

1 The effect of this design is determined to a large extent by the shape and texture of the twigs. Choose the most gnarled and weathered ones you can find. The covering of green growth on the ones we used is especially effective. Polish the apples so that they shine in the candlelight.

2 Bend a stub wire to make a U-shaped staple. Place one of the twigs flat against the ring, so the branches extend well beyond the circular shape. Press the staple over the twig and into the ring and check that the twig is held securely. Secure the remaining twigs in a similar way.

3 Push a stub wire through each apple close to the base, bring the ends together and twist them. Press the twisted wires flat against the apple.

4 Bend a stub wire in half, thread it through the wire at the base of an apple, and press the wire ends at a slanting angle into the twig ring. Check that the apple is firmly held in position. Wire on the remaining ones in a similar way, positioning some around the inside and some around the outside of the ring.

5 The completed ring will never win a prize for its neat-and-tidyness, but it will find favor with guests in a party mood. You could hang the ring over a tub of apples bobbing in water – a traditional Halloween game which is still popular.

6 An eye-catching decorative hoop which will certainly impress all who see it.

VINE WREATH

The winery harvest is a time for great celebration and, in a vintage year, is the cue for a good party. Our unusual decoration, which would be especially appropriate for an outdoor gathering, is entwined with vine leaves, hung with black and white grapes, and adorned with roses. Why roses? Some vintners plant rosebushes at the end of their vines, as an early-warning for crop damage.

1 Choose long, supple vine stems that can easily be entwined around the ring. If vines are not available, you could substitute clematis stems or another similar shrub in full leaf.

YOU WILL NEED

twisted-twig ring; ours was 12 inches in diameter

stub wires

wire cutters

flower scissors or secateurs

trails of grape leaves

bunches of black and white grapes

roses

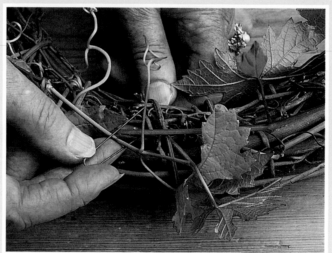

2 Cut a stub wire in half and bend it to make a U-shaped staple. Place a vine stem over the ring and push the stem end under the twig-ring binding where possible. Secure the remaining length of the stem with a wire staple. Continue around the ring until it is covered with vines.

3 Cut the grapes into small but thick bunches – you want the ring to have a look of abundance. Place the grapes over the ring so that they will hang downward in a natural way. Secure them to the twig ring by hooking a stubwire staple over the vine stem and into the ring.

4 *Secure the roses to one side of the ring (at about 11 o'clock) by threading the stems under the twig-ring binding. The juxtaposition of the full, bright pink roses and the black grapes is especially attractive.*

5 *Completely at home in its surroundings: the vine wreath hanging above a fruitful vine. The decoration would look equally good on a door, a gatepost, an outside wall, or a garden table.*

HALLOWEEN CANDLE RING

Special lighting effects make all the difference to the atmosphere created for a Halloween party, and candles are crucial. We have designed a candlestick ring composed of dried materials in weird and wonderful shapes, from spiky cereals to prickly flower heads, and in an improbable mixture of colors, taking in both mauve and orange. You could make a ring like this one to outline your own most way-out candlestick, or to encircle a glass jelly jar holding a night-light or a candle.

YOU WILL NEED

———

pre-formed dry foam ring or block of dry foam

knife

string

scissors

flower scissors

selection of dried materials, such as wheat, oats, poppy heads, straw flowers, statice, thistles

———

1 As all the dried materials are used with short pieces of stem, and as the color scheme is random rather than carefully planned, you should be able to use snippings left over from other designs. Try to include some rugged shapes, such as the thistles and carthamus.

2 If you cannot obtain a dry foam ring, you can cut one from a block of foam, using a small plate for the outline. Cut two semi-circles, butt them together and tie them around with string. Insert short pieces of oat stems around the top and outside of the ring. The inside of the ring is not decorated.

3 Fill in the design with flowers in random order. Cut some stems very short and press the flower head close against the foam. That way, you need fewer flowers to cover and conceal the foam.

4 The completed ring, with heads of wheat and stems of oats shooting off in all directions and the foam ring covered with a kaleidoscope of color. This ring is cut so the candlestick just rests on top.

5 A trio of lighting effects, with stubby red candles pressed into the top of rosy red apples (an appropriate idea for Halloween) and a night-light owl beaming approval.

RING OF OATS

It's so sensational, the way that sunlight filters through a field of oats, that we decided to recreate the effect in a purely domestic situation. Our ring of oats, which is bound with dried poppy heads for contrast, can be used as a curtain, hung above a fireplace, on a door or a plain, dark wall.

YOU WILL NEED

flat copper-wire ring; ours was 10 inches in diameter

gutta-percha tape (optional)

roll of fine silver wire

scissors

flower scissors

ribbon, 1 inch wide

dried oats

dried poppy heads

1 *Choose a ribbon color that will contrast sharply with the neutral, sun-bleached shade of the oats and seed heads. Red or blue would also be good choices.*

2 *Tie the roll wire to the outer ring. Take four or five stems of oats. Place them over the ring close to the wire, the heads facing outward. The eventual size of the decoration is determined by the length of stem you use. Take the stem ends through the center of the ring, and bend them back, in line with the stem tops. Continue binding stems around the ring. Bind poppy stems (shorter than the oats) in a similar way. Trim off excess stem ends at the back.*

3 *Cover about three-quarters of the ring with oats and poppyheads. Knot one end of the ribbon close to the stems and wind it around the inner and outer rings. Knot the ribbon close to the stems at the other end and cut it off. Tie the remaining ribbon around the top of the ring and tie it into a bow.*

4 *As you can see, the finished design would be as effective hanging above a fireplace, on a door or a plain dark wall.*

THANKSGIVING SWAG

Our Thanksgiving decoration brings together a medley of dried wheat, oats, hops, and grasses, a handful of bright hot chilies, seed heads, and dried flowers. We show the garland outlining a miniature shelf unit in the kitchen, but it is an idea you could adapt, using eggplants and Indian corn to decorate a dresser or a doorway.

1 Measure the string to drape over and around the piece of furniture to be decorated and tie a knot in it to mark the center. (To decorate a large piece of furniture, using heavy vegetables and fruits in the garland, you would need to use strong cord or rope as the core material.)

YOU WILL NEED

thick string

scissors

roll of fine silver wire

flower scissors

selection of dried wheat, oats, hops, and grasses

green and red chilies

dried flowers, such as carthamus

dried poppy heads

2 Make bunches of the dried materials, including a spray of hops, if available, in each one. Starting from the center and working outward, bind the bunches to the string, taking the roll wire over several times to secure each one. Ensure that the cereal and grass heads cover the stems of the one before.

3 Wire several chilies together by taking roll wire around and around the stems. Our choice of chilies was determined more by color and shape variation than for any culinary considerations! Bind the groups of chilies to the garland at regular intervals.

4 *When you have completed one side of the garland, start again from the center and, reversing the direction of the stems, work out toward the other side. Take care that the principal items in the design, and especially the bunches of chilies, match on both sides.*

5 *Place the garland over the unit and fix it if necessary, although usually the weight of the side trails will be enough to keep it in place. Tuck in extra materials such as a few dried flowers or sprays of hops to cover the change of direction in the center, and make good any gaps.*

CHAPTER 8

PURE NOSTALGIA

*W*reaths and garlands are so much associated with festivals and
celebrations of all kinds that it is tempting to
think of them only in those terms, and to confine the decorations to
high days and holidays – which would be a
great pity, and a waste of a wonderful opportunity for pure self-
indulgence! This section is a medley of designs
which, too, have long and happy associations – with lazy summer
days, with the romance that typifies a bygone
era, and with the unspoken language of flowers. Each of the
decorations is composed of dried flowers and
foliage, or of materials that can be left to dry on the decoration, so it
can be treasured for years to come as an item
of pure nostalgia.
Looking back wistfully to summer, and capturing
the vibrant colors and heady scents of the season, there is a wreath
covered with sweet-smelling hay and
blossoming with posies of flowers that evoke memories of a country
garden in its prime – peonies and roses among
them. Turning the focus of attention to the herb garden, and a well-
stocked one at that, there is a herb wreath
packed with the deep, rich colors and mingling aromas of a knot
garden centuries ago; but, to be practical,
it is a style you could recreate effectively with a limited selection of
herbs and flowers.
Scented plants are featured again in two designs which, although
completely different in style and concept,
have their origins in Victorian times. One, a ring covered with
potpourri, gives shape and form to the blend of
petals, flower oils, and spices that has recently enjoyed a comeback as
an environmental perfume. The other, a circlet
of lavender and pale pastel flowers, might have come straight from
great-grandmother's bottom drawer.

LAVENDER RING

A ring of lavender has gentle connotations reminiscent of a by-gone age, and would make a delightful gift for a venerable aunt or grandmother. Our design, the lavender bunches alternated with the softest, palest mauve statice, would charm the younger generation, too.

YOU WILL NEED

2 stub wires

white gutta-percha tape

scissors

roll of fine silver wire

flower scissors

ribbon, 1 inch wide

dried lavender

dried statice

1 The design is composed of a ring made of two stub wires joined together and bound around with white gutta-percha tape. It has a diameter of 7½ inches. Choose the palest color of statice you can find. If you cannot find pastel mauve, use pale pink, pale blue, or white, and choose matching ribbon.

2 Cut the lavender stems short and group them into small bunches. Bind the stems with fine roll wire for easy binding. Cut sprays of statice short and bind them into small bunches. Attach the first lavender bunch to the ring with roll wire, taking it tightly over the stems and around the ring. Do not cut.

3 Bind on statice and lavender bunches alternately, so the flower heads of one bunch cover the stems of the one before. Continue binding on flower bunches until the ring is covered. If traces of the wire ring show, tuck extra lavender or statice stems under the roll wire.

4 Tie the ribbon around the ring and over the stems. Tie it into a bow and neaten the ends by cutting them at a slanted angle.

5 *The finished design could be displayed on a dresser, hung in a closet, or placed in a drawer to scent lingerie or woolens.*

PEONY RING

The deep, hazy pink of dried peonies, the pretty luxury of dried cream-colored rosebuds, the scents of the herb garden and the sensuous feel of sun-dried hay, all come together in a design that pays a romantic tribute to summer. You could display it on a bedroom or living-room wall, on an occasional table, or in a shallow, rustic basket.

YOU WILL NEED

flat copper-wire ring; ours was
10 inches in diameter

well-dried hay or dry
sphagnum moss

twine

scissors

stub wires

flower scissors

dried peonies

dried rosebuds

dried sea lavender

dried purple sage leaves

dried poppy heads

1 Cover the ring thickly on both sides with hay, binding it around and around with twine. The way to do this is shown in the photographs on page 35. Select flowers in the romantic colors of summer: deep and pale pink and cream make a delightful combination.

2 Cut the stems of the dried flowers short. Gather them into full mixed bunches, composed of one peony, a rosebud, a poppy head, several sprays of sea lavender and several stems of sage. Bind the stems with a stub wire, and twist the two ends of the wire together.

3 To attach the bunches to the hay ring, push the wire ends deep into the hay and through to the back. Bend the wires back over the outer wire circle of the ring. Add more bunches around the ring, positioning some bunches close to the outside and others close to the inside of the ring. As usual, the flower heads of one bunch will cover and conceal the stems of the one before.

4 *The decoration is designed to leave one section of the tactile hay uncovered, but you could complete the ring by adding more bunches.*

VALENTINE HEART

The perfect gift for your partner on Valentine's Day, a wedding anniversary or a birthday, or just to say, "I love you." The design is composed on a heart-shaped twig ring and decorated with the most romantic of all floral symbols, red roses. It would look delightful hanging over a bed headboard or placed on a bedroom window seat.

YOU WILL NEED

heart-shaped twisted-twig ring

roll of fine silver wire

scissors

stub wires

wire cutters

flower scissors

lacy ribbon; ours was 2 inches wide cotton crochet

dried rosebuds

dried sea lavender

dried baby's-breath

1 You may be able to buy a heart-shaped twisted-twig ring at a florist or flower club. If not, you could make one by forming a piece of thick wire into a heart shape and covering it with supple twigs.

2 Cut the stems of the dried flowers short and make them into posies, composed of two rosebuds and a few sprays of sea lavender and baby's-breath. Bind the posy stems with roll wire. Cut stub wires in half and bend them into U-shaped staples.

3 Place a posy flat against the twig shape, with the stems following the outline. Secure the posy by pushing a wire staple over the stems and into the twigs.

4 *Add more posies to follow the heart shape, positioning them so the flowers of one posy cover and hide the stems of the one before. Reverse the direction of the stems at the base of the heart, so all the flower heads are facing toward the top of the design. Our design includes two posies featuring cream instead of red rosebuds – just to be different.*

5 *Tie the lacy ribbon into a bow and trim the ends neatly. Push a wire staple through the loop at the back, and press it into the center top of the heart.*

6 *The finished heart – designed to melt your heart.*

BLUE-AND-WHITE CIRCLET

A plain white pitcher takes on a new and more romantic personality when it is encircled by a ring of dried flowers. To flatter our lovely Parianware pitcher, we made a selection of larkspur, love-in-a-mist, ammobium, cornflowers and sea lavender, all in old-fashioned blue and white.

YOU WILL NEED

dry foam ring; ours was 6 inches in diameter; or you can make one by cutting the shape in two halves from a block of dry foam

flower scissors

dried larkspur

dried love-in-a-mist

dried ammobium

dried cornflowers

dried sea lavender

1 *The long spires of dried larkspur can be snipped into several short stems to bring them into scale with a small design. The cornflowers, still the brightest of blue, were dried in a microwave.*

2 *Cut short pieces of larkspur and position them close together all around the top and outer side of the ring, leaving the inside clear. Cut short pieces of the other flowers.*

3 *Fill in the ring with the other materials, keeping an even color balance all the way around. The design looks more natural if some stems of sea lavender, for example, extend a little beyond the circular outline to give a slightly spiky appearance.*

4 *The pitcher and its dried-flower circlet form part of a still-life group in a chimney alcove. The blue-and-white theme is echoed in pottery, and bunches of dried lady's mantle, lavender and love-in-a-mist hang beside the chest of drawers.*

POTPOURRI AND POSY RING

A bowl of potpourri, a medley of scented flower petals and tiny leaves, adds a note of nostalgia to any room, and is the most delightful of environmental perfumes. Our design takes the color, the texture and the aroma of the flower mixture and transforms them into an irresistibly pretty decoration, a ring that any romantic would treasure.

YOU WILL NEED

decorative grass-covered stem ring; ours was 7 inches in diameter

clear, quick-setting, all-purpose glue

roll of fine silver wire

ribbon, ½ inch wide

half a stub wire

potpourri, about 4 ounces

dried flowers such as rosebuds, sea lavender, feverfew

1 You can use a dried-foam ring, although it would not be as attractive as one made of natural stems and grasses. If you do use foam, be sure to select a glue which is suitable for use with plastic materials. Choose the potpourri and match the posy flowers and ribbon to the petal colors.

2 Spread a thick layer of glue on the surface of the ring, working on a small area at a time. Make sure that the glue spreads in between the hollows in the ring.

3 Press the potpourri firmly onto the glue. It is surprising how much will stick. Spread glue on the next area around the ring, press on more potpourri and so on, until the ring, including the sides, is completely covered.

4 *Gather the dried flowers into a posy and cut the stems short. Bind them with a short piece of roll wire, then tie the ribbon around them and make it into a bow. Bend the half stub wire into a U-shaped staple, push it over the posy stems and press the wire ends into the ring. Trim the ends of the ribbon by cutting them on a slant.*

5 *A hand-worked quilt is the perfect setting for this romantic and pretty potpourri ring.*

HERB WREATH

*T*o wander in a herb garden on a summer's evening, when all the myriad aromas are at their most pungent, is a delightful experience and one to savor. This colorful wreath can be composed of fresh materials and left to dry naturally, a nostalgic reminder of the scents of summer.

YOU WILL NEED

---

flat copper-wire ring; ours was 10 inches in diameter

dry sphagnum moss or you could use well-dried hay

twine

scissors

flower scissors

stub wires

selection of herbs and cottage-garden flowers, such as purple sage, sage, marjoram, fennel, cornflowers, modern pinks, love-in-a-mist flowers and seed heads, everlasting peas, lavender, veronica

---

1 *Cover the ring thickly on both sides with the moss, binding it around and around with twine. The directions for covering a ring in this way are given on page 35. Our selection of herbs and flowers was in the purple, pink, wine-red and gray range, with touches of green for contrast.*

2 *Cut the stems of the herbs and flowers short, and form them into mixed bunches. If you plan to leave the decoration to dry, you will need more bunches, to allow them to diminish in size as the moisture evaporates. Bind the stems of each bunch with a stub wire and twist the ends tightly at the back.*

3 *To position the first bunch of herbs, push the wire into the moss and through to the back of the wreath. Twist it over the outer circle of the wire ring and bend it flat.*

4 *Arrange more bunches all around the ring, keeping them close together. Position them so some flower heads face toward the inside of the wreath, and others face outward. The design should have a jagged and uneven rather than a smooth outline.*

5 *The essence of summer – the completed ring composed of a colorful and shapely blend of herbs and traditional plants.*

6 *The finished colorful wreath captures the mood of a summer evening with its combined perfume of the leaves.*

CHAPTER 9

CHRISTMAS AND NEW YEAR

An evergreen wreath on the front door to welcome visitors arriving for
a party or bring Christmas greetings; a
traditional fruit and foliage "kissing" ring hanging in the hall; an
Advent wreath flickering with the light of the
four symbolic candles; a glittering gold centerpiece for the festive table
— Christmas and the New Year inspire us to
create wreaths and garlands to celebrate the religious festival and
gladly decorate our homes.
We no longer believe, as ancient people did, that evergreen leaves
have magical powers (since they retain their
leaves when other trees are bare). But we do appreciate the ability of
evergreens, such as glossy holly, ivy, and
feathery cypress and yew, to transform our homes for the festive season
and play an attractive and long-lasting role in
the decorative scheme.
Many of the designs in this section are
unashamedly traditional, interpretations of decorations that have
become an essential part of the family Christmas
in many countries of the world. Our welcome wreath, composed of a
moss-covered ring and displayed on a berry-red
front door, contrasts the shiny brightness of holly and ivy with the
neutral coloring and matt texture of large
poppy seed heads, bunches of cinnamon sticks and pine cones, and adds
a finishing flourish of red tartan ribbon bows.
Red and green, the traditional colors of Christmas, are featured
again in our version of a kissing ring, hanging
on brilliant scarlet ribbons, entwined with trails of ivy and
unconventionally decorated with "designer"
apples and unseasonable strawberries.

WELCOME WREATH

A colorful wreath of evergreens and other natural materials hanging on the front door gives a warm welcome to guests through Christmas and the New Year.

YOU WILL NEED

flat copper-wire ring; ours was
10 inches in diameter

well-dried hay or sphagnum moss

twine

stub wires

wire cutters

flower scissors

raffia

ribbon, 1¼ inches wide

scissors

selection of evergreens, such
as holly, ivy and mistletoe

dried poppy heads

cinnamon sticks

small pine cones

1 Cover the wire ring thickly on both sides with hay or moss. The method is described on page 35. Select short, full sprays of evergreens to give a variety of leaf shape and texture, and include some high-gloss materials, such as holly or ivy, to give the design sparkle.

2 To make a hook for hanging, bend a stub wire to make a circular shape in the center, and twist the two ends beneath it. Push the two ends of the wire into the wreath and twist them around the outer ring of the wire frame. The hook will be covered by the evergreens at the top of the design, so it is not necessary to cover it. You could, however, cover the stub wire with gutta-percha tape before shaping it.

3 Attach all the materials even the evergreen sprays, to wires before inserting them in the wreath. Twist half a stub wire around each stem, leaving a false stem to insert in the wreath. Wrap a stub wire around the lowest ring of scales on each cone and twist it underneath. Cut the cinnamon sticks in half, wrap them around the center with a stub wire and tie raffia to cover it.

4 Push the wired materials into and through the wreath and bend the wire stalk over at the back, so it is held firm against the wire ring frame. Build up the design so that the poppy heads, cinnamon sticks and cones are evenly distributed around the ring.

5 Tie two ribbon bows, one with long trailing ends for the top of the wreath and the other flat. Bend half a stub wire in a U-shape, push it through the loop of the back of each bow, and insert it in the wreath. Neaten the ends of the ribbon by cutting them into inverted V-shapes.

6 This beautiful wreath is the ideal way to put visitors at their ease, especially hanging against a lovely wooden door.

ADVENT RING

The tradition in the Christian church, of lighting one candle on each of the four Sundays of Advent, is brought into the home with this ring, composed of winter green, white and silver dried materials.

1 Unusually, this design uses an absorbent foam ring, unsoaked, instead of a dry foam one, with mainly dried flowers. Cut the sea lavender, honesty, and mistletoe into short sprays, and make bunches of the white ammobium, wrapping the short stems with half a stub wire.

YOU WILL NEED

---

absorbent foam ring; ours was 10 inches in diameter

stub wires

wire cutters

4 plastic candle-holding holders

ribbon, 1¼ inches wide

4 candles

flower scissors

dried sea lavender

dried honesty

dried straw flowers

mistletoe

2 Press the candle holders into the foam at equal distances around the ring. Tie a ribbon around the base of the ring, to partially conceal it. The knot in the ribbon will be covered by the decorative bow.

HINT

Take care that the candles do not burn down too close to the dried materials. Do not leave the lighted decoration in a room where young children or animals are left unattended.

3 Arrange short sprays of sea lavender all around the ring so they extend over the inner and outer rims. The sea lavender serves as a background against which the other more high-profile materials will be seen.

4 Fill the design with short sprays of honesty and mistletoe, and bunches of ammobium. Turn the ring around and check that there are no gaps which allow the foam to show through. If there are, add more sprays. Make a bow from the contrasting ribbon. Bend half a stub wire into a U-shape and push it through the loop at the back of the bow. Press the wire into the foam ring so the bow covers the knot in the encircling ribbon.

HINT

It is not advisable to press thick candles (the ones in our design are 1 inch in diameter) directly into the foam, as they may break it up. If you cannot obtain the type of candle holders we show, you can make "stilts" of matchsticks or cocktail sticks to support the candle and press into the foam. Tape four sticks around the base of each candle, leaving about 1 inch extending beneath it. Push the matchsticks into the foam so the candle just rests on the surface.

KISSING RING

A kissing ring of evergreens combined with berry-bright fruits is a traditional decoration to hang over the table or in the hall at Christmastime. Here it is interpreted with "designer" fruits, but it could equally well be made with small rosy apples or with satsumas.

YOU WILL NEED

---

twisted-twig ring; ours was
12 inches in diameter

tape measure

stub wires

wire cutters

flower scissors

ribbon, 1½ inches wide

scissors

trails of ivy

real or artificial fruits

1 Long trails of ivy are the perfect choice to make the evergreen wreath because they can so easily be twined around the ring. The fruits we chose were artificial apples and (not quite in scale) equally bright strawberries.

2 Measure around the circumference of the ring to ascertain the distance between each fruit. If the fruit has a hanging loop, as ours had, it is simple to hang it on a stub-wire hook. Cut a stub wire in half, bend it into a U-shape, push it through the loop and insert the two ends of the wire in the underside of the twig ring.

3 Wind trails of ivy around the twig ring, taking them over and over the ring. Secure each stem end with a bent stub-wire staple. Check that the ivy is evenly distributed, and bind on extra trails or staple in individual leaves if there are gaps.

4 *Tie a short piece of ribbon around the twig ring, making a double knot at the top. Thread a long piece of ribbon through it, to hang the decoration. Repeat this twice more.*

5 *Make four ribbon bows, three to fix to the ring and one to fix at the top. Attach, using bent stub-wire staples.*

6 *Join the six ends of ribbon hangings at the top (you could use a pin, safety-pin, or staples), and fix the decoration where it is to hang. Attach the fourth ribbon bow at the top.*

GOLDEN NUT RING

All that glisters may not be gold, but at Christmastime it is a valuable asset to have on the table. This decorative twig ring is embellished with gilded nuts and cones, and others in their natural state by way of attractive contrast. The design is almost unbelievably quick to make, and can be assembled at the eleventh hour.

1 Choose the most decorative twig ring you can find or make your own. This one is in unbleached, twisted willow, and has just the right kind of indentations and cavities needed to take the nuts. Make your selection of nuts as varied as possible.

YOU WILL NEED

---

willow twig ring; ours was 10 inches in diameter

ozone-friendly gold aerosol spray

clear, quick-setting, all-purpose glue

ribbons, ½ inch and 1¼ inches wide

scissors

stub wires

wire cutters

selection of nuts, such as pecans, almonds, walnuts, chestnuts, brazils

small pine cones

2 Cover the working surface with paper and select the nuts and cones to be gilded. Spray them on one side, leave them to dry, then turn them over and spray them on the other side. Leave them to dry again.

3 Squeeze a generous amount of glue onto the base of each nut and cone, press it onto the ring and hold it in place for a few moments while the glue sets. Alternate the sprayed materials with the natural ones to achieve a good color balance.

4 *Cut two pieces of the narrower ribbon. Cut a stub wire in half, wrap it around the center of the ribbons, and press the ends of the wire into the ring. Make a bow from the wider ribbon, bend half a stub wire into a U shape, thread it through the loop at the back of the bow, and fix it to the ring.*

5 *The warm and glistening colors on this decorative twig ring are certainly an asset to any dining table.*

CHILDREN'S CANDY RING

Here's a ring that will bring a sparkle to the children's eyes! And older children will delight in helping to make it. Perhaps it is worth noting that the candies have been counted – there are four in each paper-doily cone!

YOU WILL NEED

large flat plate

small shallow dish

block of absorbent foam

knife

string

scissors

6 paper doilies, 7½ inches in diameter

stub wires

wire cutters

flower scissors

ribbons, ½ inch wide

sprays of evergreen, such as juniper or cypress

brightly wrapped candies

1 Outline the flat plate with slices of soaked absorbent foam and tie around the foam with string. Choose evergreens that have a feathery outline. The one shown is juniper.

2 Make a cone shape from each of the paper doilies. Fold a doily into half, and half again, to give a quarter segment, and then pinch the cone to make a point. Wrap half a stub wire tightly around the point.

3 Arrange the doilies evenly around the ring, pushing the wire into the foam. Ease out the paper to make full, open cone shapes. Cut short sprays of evergreen and insert them into the foam, between the doilies, until all the spaces are filled and the foam blocks are completely hidden.

4 Cut the stub wires in half and twist one around the wrappings of each of the candies. Fill the paper cones with candies by pushing the wires through the holes on the doilies.

5 Cut equal pieces of ribbons, wrap half a stub wire around the center and push the wire into the foam. Cut the ribbon ends on a slant. Fill the dish in the center of the design with more candies. As the wires do not pierce the candies at all, the goodies will be safe to eat when the design is dismantled.

BERRY GARLAND

An evergreen garland studded with true or false berries makes a seasonal decoration for a footed plate, a pedestal dish or a compote. The dish could display an arrangement of pomanders and nuts, Christmas cookies, or plum pudding.

YOU WILL NEED

pedestal dish

thick wire

roll of fine silver wire

ribbon, ¼ inch wide

sprays of evergreens, such as ivy and box

false berries

1 *Cut a piece of wire to go around the circumference of the dish and, if you like, make a hook and eye at the ends. Glossy evergreens are the best choice for a decorative garland of this kind. We contrasted dark, heavily veined ivy leaves with suitably slender sprays of lighter green box.*

2 *It's a horticultural phenomenon: sprays of box resplendent with glowing red berries. Wind several berries onto each evergreen spray so they make a real impact.*

3 *Using the roll wire, bind ivy and box sprays together onto the wire ring. Bind successive sprays so they cover the stems of the ones before. Continue binding on more evergreens all around the ring until it is completely covered.*

4 *Cut off a piece of ribbon to make a bow. Cut the remainder into three equal pieces and, using them together, bind them over and around the evergreens leaving the ribbons loose, so they make gentle folds. Tie the ribbon ends where they meet, and cover the knot with a ribbon bow.*

5 *Fix the evergreen garland over the dish and cut off any stray stems or prominent leaves that look out of place.*

HERBAL GIFT RINGS

Make aromatic rings from fresh or dried herbs and present them as unusual and thoughtful gifts to cooking-loving friends. You can follow our example and use rosemary, purple sage and marjoram individually, or take several herbs together and include perhaps, bay, fennel seedheads and others.

YOU WILL NEED

---

wire rings; ours were 7 inches in diameter

roll of fine silver wire

scissors

flower scissors

selection of ribbons

rosemary leaves

purple sage leaves

marjoram flowers

1 We used ready-made copper rings, but you could make them by joining two stub wires together to form a circle. You can, if you wish, bind the wire circles with gutta-percha tape before decorating them with the herbs.

2 Take several short stems of rosemary together, wrap them around the wire ring and bind them tightly with the roll wire. Add more stems and bind them on to the ring all the way around, until it is covered. Cover another ring with short sprays of purple sage leaves in a similar way.

3 The third ring is covered with mauve and white marjoram flowers. You can use fresh flowers and leave them to dry attractively on the ring, or use flowers which have already been dried. Finish each ring with a small, decorative bow of festive ribbon.

4 *The herbal rings are shown as part of a culinary, and highly aromatic, gift basket. The rosemary ring is tied to the basket handle, the marjoram ring frames a pile of rosy apples, and the sage ring is in the foreground. Stems of dried fennel are grouped at the back of the basket.*

INDEX

Page references in *italics* refer to captions to illustrations